Praise for
Jesus Followers

"For Christian parents, there's no task more important than handing down our faith to the next generation. In *Jesus Followers,* Anne Graham Lotz and her daughter Rachel-Ruth show us what it looks like to model a vibrant, contagious faith so that our children might ultimately embrace Christ too."
—JIM DALY, president of Focus on the Family

"Anne and Rachel-Ruth have produced an engaging and practical book that will encourage you to live out your walk with God in a manner that motivates your children and grandchildren to follow your example. Drawing from one of the world's most famous Christian families, this book is filled with inspiring and delightful stories. Best of all, you'll realize as you read that you don't have to be Billy and Ruth Graham to raise godly children, as long as you embrace the wisdom and guidance of their God!"
—RICHARD BLACKABY, coauthor of *Experiencing God* and *Experiencing God at Home*

"Standing firm against cultural trends in order to raise up Jesus Followers has never been more challenging—or more urgently needed. Which is why I'm thankful that, through unforgettable family stories and biblical examples, Anne Graham Lotz and Rachel-Ruth Lotz Wright have crafted an inspiring guide for living with intentionality and instilling truth in the next generation."
—DR. TONY EVANS, president of the Urban Alternative and senior pastor of Oak Cliff Bible Fellowship

"Many Christian families today would like to leave a legacy of faith for the next generation but sadly lack any example of what this looks like. *Jesus Followers* offers the example we all need, giving us a beautiful, honest look at what a legacy of faith can look like when a family chooses to truly follow Jesus. My faith has been ignited by every chapter of this book!"
—MONICA SWANSON, author of *Boy Mom* and host of the *Boy Mom* podcast

"How can we raise godly children in a godless culture? Anne and her daughter Rachel-Ruth answer this growing dilemma through powerful stories and biblical principles to equip and inspire you to develop Jesus Followers in your own family. From heartfelt laughter to tearful accounts of life's tragedies, their book reveals how God helps us draw near to Him and help those we love. They tackle everything from discussions of purity and marriage to facing the everyday storms of life, challenging you to invest in the lives of your children so they can impact their children and future generations."
—Dr. John Ankerberg, founder and president of
The John Ankerberg Show (jashow.org)

"In this brilliant book, Anne Graham Lotz and Rachel-Ruth Lotz Wright invite us into their family's story, and along the way, we find many important and inspiring teaching moments for our own lives. Throughout these wonderfully wise chapters, we're encouraged to walk in grace, worship with joy, bring faith to the home and workplace, and trust in God in every situation. But most refreshing of all, we are invited into a wholehearted, vibrant relationship with Jesus Christ. Highly recommended!"
—Matt and Beth Redman, singer-songwriters
and worship leaders

"For those of us raised in Christian homes, as well as those who have had no model, this book is a godsend. Anne and Rachel-Ruth have conveyed God's clear call and instruction, along with practical examples for passing the Baton. I finished this book convinced that I can and *must* pass it on well!"
—Clyde Christensen, quarterbacks coach for the
Tampa Bay Buccaneers

"Each new generation needs to hear the gospel. Billy Graham preached the gospel faithfully to his generation. His daughter Anne has carried the baton of faith to reach her generation. And now she and her daughter Rachel-Ruth Lotz Wright are helping us know how to reach the next generation. Their new book, *Jesus Followers,* will help you take stock of your faith and grow in your walk with Christ. I highly recommend it."
—Greg Laurie, senior pastor of Harvest Christian Fellowship

Jesus Followers

Jesus
Followers

Real-Life Lessons
for Igniting Faith
in the Next Generation

Anne
Graham
Lotz
and
Rachel–Ruth
Lotz
Wright

MULTNOMAH

JESUS FOLLOWERS

Published in the United States by Multnomah, an imprint of Random House, a division of Penguin Random House LLC.

MULTNOMAH® and its mountain colophon are registered trademarks of Penguin Random House LLC.

Author is represented by Alive Literary Agency, 7680 Goddard Street, Suite 200, Colorado Springs, Colorado 80920, www.aliveliterary.com.

LIBRARY OF CONGRESS CATALOGING-IN-PUBLICATION DATA
Names: Lotz, Anne Graham, 1948- author. | Wright, Rachel-Ruth Lotz, author.
Title: Jesus followers : real-life lessons for igniting faith in the next generation / Anne Graham Lotz and Rachel-Ruth Lotz Wright.
Description: Colorado Springs, Colorado : Multnomah, [2021] | Includes bibliographical references.
Identifiers: LCCN 2021025595 | ISBN 9780525651208 (hardcover) | ISBN 9780525651390 (ebook)
Subjects: LCSH: Witness bearing (Christianity) | Christian education of children. | Families—Religious life.
Classification: LCC BV4520 .L57 2021 | DDC 248.4—dc23
LC record available at https://lccn.loc.gov/2021025595

Printed in the United States of America on acid-free paper

waterbrookmultnomah.com

2 4 6 8 9 7 5 3 1

First Edition

Book design by Susan Turner

SPECIAL SALES Most Multnomah books are available at special quantity discounts when purchased in bulk by corporations, organizations, and special-interest groups. Custom imprinting or excerpting can also be done to fit special needs. For information, please email specialmarketscms@penguinrandomhouse.com.

Dedicated
to
Bell, Sophia, and Riggin
and
to the parents and grandparents of the next generation

I will establish my covenant as an everlasting covenant
between me and you and your descendants after you
for the generations to come,
to be your God
and
the God of your descendants after you.

Genesis 17:7

CONTENTS

INTRODUCTION

The Race of Life

Almost every weekend during the spring months, my husband, Danny, would take our three young children to watch the track-and-field events at the University of North Carolina, which was his alma mater.

One of their favorite events was the four-by-one-hundred-meter relay race, in which four runners compete as a team. The race is still one of our favorite Olympic track events! As it begins, the first runner from each team crouches at the starting block, gripping the baton. When the signal is given, the runner explodes out of the starting block and runs the first hundred meters as swiftly as he can. As he completes his lap around the track, he approaches the second runner on his team. The second runner is already in full stride when the first runner reaches out and passes the baton to his teammate, who continues running at full speed in front of him. The second runner then runs his hundred-meter lap and passes the baton to the number three runner, who takes it in full stride, and so on until the fourth runner crosses the finish line, clutching the all-important baton.

Winning a relay race depends not only on the speed of the runners but also on each team member's ability to transfer the baton. If the baton is dropped or even bobbled, precious seconds are wasted, and the race may be lost. If the runner fails to pass the baton, the team is disqualified from the race altogether.

You and I are in a race called life. The Baton is Truth that leads to faith in Jesus Christ. Each generation receives the Baton from the previous generation, runs the race to the best of its ability, then is responsible for passing it smoothly and securely to the next generation.

Passing the Baton of Truth traces all the way back to the first generation of humanity. Following Adam and Eve's disobedience, when sin entered the human race, each person faced the decision of whether to seek a right relationship with God or pursue his or her own selfish desires. In Genesis 5, we find a genealogy that lists ten generations and reveals the passing of the Baton from one to the next. Each man listed lived in the midst of a civilization dominated by Cain's attitude of defiance toward God. The civilization was so wicked that it provoked God's judgment, resulting in the Flood.

Amid the wickedness of Cain's civilization, these ten men stood out like giants surrounded by spiritual dwarfs. Like a ten-man relay team, each received the Baton of Truth from the one who had preceded him. It is interesting to note that each generation was represented by a named individual, not a couple. Could it be that some of these individuals were single parents? While we can't know for certain, we do know that each received the Baton, then grasped it for himself, running his own race with diligence and perseverance. Regardless of whether or not they had believing spouses . . . regardless of their wicked surroundings . . . these individuals successfully passed Truth to the next generation.

Like Cain's civilization, ours is experiencing a bankruptcy of moral and spiritual values that threatens to erode our very existence. The flashing-red-light warning for you and me is to beware of . . .

getting caught up in the way everyone around us is acting . . .

indulging in self-pity or self-focus as struggling parents, single or otherwise . . .

living for our own selfish desires and happiness . . .

conforming to the pressure of the opinions of others . . .

succumbing to the fear of our cancel-culture . . .

and thus neglect to pass Truth to our children.

As parents, grandparents, and mentors, we must strive to be giants among spiritual dwarfs by receiving, running with, and relaying to the next generation the Baton of Truth that leads to personal faith in Jesus Christ.

In order to be successful, it's imperative that we be genuine Jesus Followers ourselves. And that's why I felt compelled to write this book with my daughter Rachel-Ruth.

Drawing on the Genesis 5 genealogy as a framework, the pages that follow are divided into four parts to reflect the four-by-one-hundred-meter relay race and expand on the biblical description of the very first transfers of the Baton. These transfers seem to emphasize the unique impact of our witness, our worship, our walk, and our work, all of which lead to a smooth, successful passing of the Baton. Rachel-Ruth illustrates each segment in the race of life by sharing stories from our family, offering vivid descriptions of how the Baton was passed to us, inspiring us to live in such a way that we can effectively pass it to those who follow.

Our hope is to encourage you to be intentional as you, too, seek to be a Jesus Follower who successfully passes the Baton to the next generation.

Genesis 5

The Beginning of the Race

¹This is the book of the genealogy of Adam. In the day that God created man, He made him in the likeness of God. ²He created them male and female, and blessed them and called them Mankind in the day they were created. ³And Adam lived one hundred and thirty years, and begot a son in his own likeness, after his image, and named him Seth. ⁴After he begot Seth, the days of Adam were eight hundred years; and he had sons and daughters. ⁵So all the days that Adam lived were nine hundred and thirty years; and he died.

⁶Seth lived one hundred and five years, and begot Enosh. ⁷After he begot Enosh, Seth lived eight hundred and seven years, and had sons and daughters. ⁸So all the days of Seth were nine hundred and twelve years; and he died.

⁹Enosh lived ninety years, and begot Cainan. ¹⁰After he begot Cainan, Enosh lived eight hundred and fifteen years, and had sons and daughters. ¹¹So all the days of Enosh were nine hundred and five years; and he died.

¹²Cainan lived seventy years, and begot Mahalalel. ¹³After he begot Mahalalel, Cainan lived eight hundred and forty years, and

had sons and daughters. [14]So all the days of Cainan were nine hundred and ten years; and he died.

[15]Mahalalel lived sixty-five years, and begot Jared. [16]After he begot Jared, Mahalalel lived eight hundred and thirty years, and had sons and daughters. [17]So all the days of Mahalalel were eight hundred and ninety-five years; and he died.

[18]Jared lived one hundred and sixty-two years, and begot Enoch. [19]After he begot Enoch, Jared lived eight hundred years, and had sons and daughters. [20]So all the days of Jared were nine hundred and sixty-two years; and he died.

[21]Enoch lived sixty-five years, and begot Methuselah. [22]After he begot Methuselah, Enoch walked with God three hundred years, and had sons and daughters. [23]So all the days of Enoch were three hundred and sixty-five years. [24]And Enoch walked with God; and he was not, for God took him.

[25]Methuselah lived one hundred and eighty-seven years, and begot Lamech. [26]After he begot Lamech, Methuselah lived seven hundred and eighty-two years, and had sons and daughters. [27]So all the days of Methuselah were nine hundred and sixty-nine years; and he died.

[28]Lamech lived one hundred and eighty-two years, and had a son. [29]And he called his name Noah, saying, "This one will comfort us concerning our work and the toil of our hands, because of the ground which the LORD has cursed." [30]After he begot Noah, Lamech lived five hundred and ninety-five years, and had sons and daughters. [31]So all the days of Lamech were seven hundred and seventy-seven years; and he died.

[32]And Noah was five hundred years old, and Noah begot Shem, Ham, and Japheth.[1]

PART ONE

Our Witness

By faith Abel offered God a better sacrifice than Cain did. By faith he was commended as a righteous man, when God spoke well of his offerings. And by faith he still speaks, even though he is dead.

Hebrews 11:4

The Bible states in Genesis 1 that in the beginning God created everything. *Everything!* Day by day by day, He brought everything into existence where nothing had existed previously. On the sixth day of Creation, God created people in His own image with the capacity to have a personal relationship with Him. And that's when the race of life began—in the Garden of Eden with our first parents, Adam and Eve.

While Genesis 1 offers a telescopic view of creation, chapter 2 presents a more detailed view.

The Baton Is Received Face to Face

In Genesis 2, we find that God created the first man of the dust of the ground. He breathed His own life into him, and the man became a living person. And then God created woman from man and gave the woman, Eve, to the man, Adam. So Adam and Eve lived together in the Garden of Eden in the visible presence of God.

Think about it. They knew God face to face. They knew the sound of His voice. They knew the touch of His hand. They saw the light in His eyes when He was with them. They saw the expression on His face when He was talking. They witnessed His strength and wisdom as He worked side by side with them. They knew God in a personal relationship. They knew firsthand that He was real, He was alive, and He was present in their lives. This was paradise. This was the Garden of Eden. This was their home.

Then the darkness of death and evil crept into the glory of creation and the perfection of paradise. The devil disguised himself as a snake that slithered up to Eve, tempting her to doubt God's word, then disobey what God had said. She fell for the temptation and led her husband, Adam, to do the same. As a result, sin entered the human race.

The snake had said that if they disobeyed God, they would be like Him in that they would know good and evil.[1] Following their sin, they knew good because they were separated from it. They knew evil because they were saturated in it.[2] Tragically, all who followed were born with a sin nature, which separates people from God to this very day.

In judgment for their disobedience, God removed Adam and Eve from the Garden of Eden. A holy God could no longer have fellowship with His beloved children, who had been created by Him and for Him.[3] Their sin was a barrier.

The Baton Is Relayed Faith to Faith

Genesis doesn't give us details, but God must have told Adam and Eve that they could come back to Him by faith through a blood sacrifice. Later, His law clearly revealed that without the shedding of blood, there would be no forgiveness.[4] All the sin offerings in the Old Testament were visual aids that pointed to the Lamb of God,[5] who one day would be sacrificed on the cross to make atonement for sin. Each time someone presented a sacrifice in the Old Testament, it was as though God said, "I owe you forgiveness." The New Testament tells us that the blood of animals cannot take away sin, but Jesus did! His sacrifice, foreshadowed so long ago in the Garden of Eden, paid all the IOU notes in full.[6]

The requirement of a blood sacrifice seems to have been clearly communicated to Adam and Eve, because their second son, Abel, chose to approach God in that way and God commended him for it. Abel chose to receive the Baton.

There is no record of Abel teaching or preaching. At this early stage of history, there may have been few other people. Instead, he seems to have silently lived a righteous life that was very different from that of his brother Cain. Abel's witness has stood the test of time, influencing those who have followed, including you and me.

What caused Abel to choose to be a righteous man? I wonder if it was the positive example of his own father within the home. Did Adam's absolute confidence in the reality of God influence his son?

Surely, although he was now separated from Him, Adam never forgot the touch of God's hand, the sound of God's voice, the expressions on God's face, the authority of God's spoken word. His faith in who God is and what God had said would have been unshakable because he knew God firsthand.

The Baton of Truth was relayed also to me by a positive example of faith within the home.

My own parents were so confident in who God is and what God has said that it never crossed my mind—nor, to my knowledge, the minds of my siblings—to doubt either God's existence or God's Word.

Both of my parents were raised by parents who were confident in God. My maternal grandparents were so confident in who God is and what God has said that they left everything in order to devote twenty-five years of their lives to establishing a hospital and caring for people in mainland China. Later, when they were forced out of China by the Japanese and returned home to the United States, my grandfather established himself as a highly respected church leader and helped found two national Christian magazines.[7]

My paternal grandparents were so confident in who God is and what God has said that my grandmother taught a weekly Bible study in their home and my grandfather was instrumental in beginning rescue missions all across the country. My grandfather also met with other men in his city to pray that God would raise up an evangelist to the world, never dreaming that God's answer would be his own son.

Who has impressed you with his or her confidence in God? What a blessing to have parents and grandparents with confident faith. What a blessing to be a parent or grandparent with confident faith!

Whether or not it was Adam's example that inspired Abel, we do know that Abel made his own decision to live a righteous life. His decision to bring a blood sacrifice, when his brother Cain gave God whatever he felt like giving, revealed his receptivity to the truth and his obedience to God's word.[8] Although he lived with parents who had rebelled against God and with a brother who was defiant, angry, and belligerent,[9] Abel turned to God.

While we need to speak up and share the truth,[10] a witness that is lived may be even more powerful than one that is spoken. It's not just what you and I say but who we are that catches the attention of those around us. As you read Rachel-Ruth's stories, this truth will be fleshed out in living color.

Abel's righteous witness provoked anger and jealousy in his brother Cain, who then rose up and murdered him. Abel's choice to live by faith in God was a silent witness for which he paid the ultimate price. Yet in doing so, he effectively passed the Baton to the next generation. It was for this witness that the writer to the Hebrews singled him out for commendation, saying, "By faith he still speaks, even though he is dead."[11] Abel's life, although brief, was not wasted. His faith in God, expressed through his silent witness, secured him an honored place in Hebrews 11, which is often referred to as the Hall of Faith.

Although to our knowledge Abel never married or had children, he did have a younger brother, born after he was murdered. Adam and Eve named this younger brother Seth, which means "appointed," because, as Eve said, "God has granted me another child in place of Abel, since Cain killed him."[12] Surely, as little Seth grew up, he was told about his two older brothers . . . about the lives they had lived . . . about the choices they had made. As a result, Seth chose to receive the Baton of Truth and passed it to his son Enosh.

What will people think of you when you're gone? What will your grandchildren know about you? Perhaps you see shadows of this ancient generation in your own family tree as you consider those who chose faith and those who did not. Wouldn't it be wonderful if, like Abel, you are remembered throughout generations to come as one whose life bore unmistakable witness to your faith in God? The choice is yours.

The following stories have been written to encourage and challenge you to think through the legacy you are building. The stories are written from Rachel-Ruth's perspective, drawing on her firsthand knowledge of parents and grandparents, and in them, you will learn about the powerful witness of previous generations that has borne rich fruit in her life. We pray you will be blessed.

1

Making the Most of Every Opportunity

Anyone familiar with Billy Graham—known to my family as Daddy Bill—knows he shared his faith boldly, without hesitation. Whether witnessing to individuals or preaching in a crowded arena, he did not speak with rehearsed precision. He spoke with passion and conviction because he believed every word he said with every fiber of his being! His deep love for Jesus was always evident in the fire in his piercing blue eyes and the passionate conviction in his familiar voice.

Thousands, even millions, came to faith in Jesus because Daddy Bill's passionate heart for the gospel came through in everything he said and did. Nothing brought him more joy than seeing someone come to Christ! My grandmother, whom we called Tai Tai, told my mom that she and Daddy Bill were once the guests of some friends at a beautiful beach resort. At dinnertime, no one could find Daddy Bill. When Tai Tai went looking for him, she found him behind their building, sharing the gospel with one of the groundskeepers.

My paternal grandfather, whom we simply called Grampa, also

shared the gospel with everyone with whom he came in contact, whether a pedestrian on a street corner in New York City, the person riding next to him on the subway, the waiter at the delicatessen he frequented, or one of the hitchhikers he often picked up for the sole purpose of sharing the gospel with them.

One Thanksgiving he and Gramma were driving down from New York City to spend a week with us. Mom had fixed a beautiful meal to enjoy upon their arrival. We waited and waited. When they finally arrived about eight hours later than expected, we learned Grampa had picked up a hitchhiker, then driven the guy to his destination— six hours out of the way—because Grampa wanted him to know Jesus!

He would say he "didn't give a rip" about what people thought of him; he cared only about what Jesus thought of him. When we get to Heaven, I can't wait to meet all the people whom he led to Christ. At Grampa's funeral, a man told my dad he had seen the notice of Grampa's death in the paper and had come to the service because he wanted the family to know that Grampa had led him to Christ at the local McDonald's, where Grampa went every morning for a cup of coffee.

It's clear that the witness of my grandparents made an impact on both of my parents, instilling in them the importance of sharing the gospel at every opportunity.

When I was in elementary school, each Christmas my mom would come in to share the gospel through the Christmas story. I attended a public school that did not look favorably on the Bible or any type of Christian teaching. To share the Christmas story openly without using a Bible, my mom had to be creative. She had the clever idea of using the encyclopedia. As she sat surrounded by my classmates, teachers congregated in the doorway and the principal made a show of being present. But no one could argue with what the encyclopedia said about Bethlehem, the angels, baby Jesus, Mary, and Joseph. While writing this, I took a moment to look up the words *Jesus, Mary, Joseph, angel, cross, forgiveness, resurrection, heaven, eternity,* and *peace* in the dictionary. And do you know what? The same thing is true! The explanations are right there. You can share the gospel from the dictionary! Try it the next time you feel led to share the gospel and someone tells you not to read the Bible in a public setting. Just thinking about it makes me smile.

The Lord has used my mom to share the gospel with many others over the years, including when she led Just Give Me Jesus revivals worldwide in large arenas. She always shared the gospel in the opening session, inviting people to come to the cross and pray with her to receive Christ. Over the years, hundreds of people streamed down to the platform. Her Friday night message on the Cross is the most powerful message I have ever heard. At every revival my mom not only focused on the audience but also had a burden for the production crew—the guys who worked behind the scenes with the lighting, the audio and video equipment, and the stage.

I remember one revival in particular that took place in the San Diego Sports Arena. The revival began Friday evening, then went all day Saturday, which also happened to be Mom's birthday. She gave three sixty-minute messages, emceed the program, then stayed almost two hours after the conclusion to greet people who lined up to speak and pray with her.

We had arranged to meet some special friends for her birthday dinner in La Jolla. She was to come straight to the restaurant from the arena. We waited and waited and waited. We finally went ahead and ordered our dinner. After we finished eating, Mom came in. We could all tell she was totally wiped out, but the sparkle in her eyes let us know she had been up to something special. And then she told us. As she was getting ready to leave the arena, she asked the guy who had handled her audio for the last five revivals whether he knew that his sins were forgiven and that he would be going to Heaven. He answered, "I'm not sure," to which Mom replied, "Would you like to make sure now?" He said yes! So Mom returned to the arena, sat down with him to answer his questions, then prayed with him as he confessed his sin, asked God to forgive him, and invited Jesus into his heart. Mom said it was the best birthday present she could have ever received.

And then there's my dad. When he wasn't talking about the Lord, he was talking about the Yankees or football or Carolina basketball or a difficult patient he encountered in his work as a dentist. Dad just loved to talk. Many men were drawn to my dad because he was a big manly guy who would shoot straight with them. He told it like it was, whatever it was, just like the New Yorker that he was. He led several men's Bible studies, and he would randomly call on guys to answer questions, which meant they all came prepared every week for fear of embarrassment! Many men came to Christ in his Bible studies. Dad's faithfulness in leading was especially apparent the week that Hurricane Fran roared through our city, destroying the electrical grid and mangling the telephone wires. He walked the three miles to his Friday morning Bible study, found no one there, and never let the guys forget that they didn't show up when he did!

Sharing the gospel is not just for the evangelists and pastors of the world, like my grandfathers, or for Bible teachers and study group leaders, like my parents. Those who have placed their faith in Jesus are called to go and tell the good news to everyone: neighbors, cab drivers, professors, plumbers, coworkers, friends, family, and the list goes on.

I've been raised in a family where telling people about Jesus is as common as drinking water. My husband, Steven, and I have tried to instill that same priority in our three girls. They feel confident in sharing the gospel because they've seen me sharing the gospel just as I've seen my parents and grandparents sharing the gospel. Hardly a day goes by when I'm not trying to talk about Jesus or His Word with someone in my path. I'm not telling people about Jesus out of a weighty sense of duty. Sharing the gospel is not about reciting a rehearsed speech, performing a mechanical exercise, or repeating some formula. I talk about Jesus because I love Him! God's Word says, "Out of the overflow of his heart his mouth speaks."[1] God's love should flow out of our hearts, compelling us to share it with others in our everyday lives. So what does that look like?

My girls have shared the gospel with friends through text messages, with classmates at school, and with teammates on the practice field. They tell people about Jesus because they love Him.

My middle daughter, Sophia, had a high school tennis match at an opposing high school one hot September day. We took our puppy, Sader, along. He needed to get his wiggles out, and my youngest daughter, Riggin, was happy to oblige. Riggin has never met a stranger. She will talk your ears off! She is full of personality and loves the Lord with all her heart. She had already shared the gospel with multiple people in her young life. That day she noticed another girl who, like Riggin, was about ten years old and who also was there to watch her sister play tennis. They immediately struck up a conversation and began to walk Sader in the grass outside the tennis courts.

The two girls never stopped talking and never stopped walking. They even carried the puppy when he got tired as they continued to walk and talk. Over two hours went by. The tennis match ended, and I motioned for Riggin to head to the car. The girls hugged, smiled, and waved goodbye like dear friends. When Riggin jumped in the car, she exclaimed, "Mom, I just led Jane to Jesus!"[2] We all screamed with excitement! She explained that as they walked around the tennis courts, she began to tell her new friend all about Heaven. Riggin said the girl asked her a ton of questions, which she answered as best she could. She then asked whether Jane wanted to make sure she was going to Heaven one day and whether she wanted her sins forgiven. The girl responded, "Of course!" So Riggin stopped and prayed with her on the spot. To this day, they are close friends. Her mother has also become one of my dearest friends.

On another occasion, we were in Florida, visiting my husband's family. My mother-in-law and I took my girls and my five-year-old niece, Annelise, to the Mall at Millenia on the south end of Orlando. It took us over thirty minutes to get there through traffic, which ended up being a divinely appointed drive. Riggin and Annelise were in the very back of the car. I knew they were talking the whole ride, but I couldn't hear what they were saying. When we got to the parking lot,

Bell and Sophia, who had been listening from the middle row of seats, and Riggin, who was in the back row, started cheering and crying. Then Riggin explained to my mother-in-law and me that she had just prayed with Annelise, who asked Jesus to come into her heart. While driving to the mall!

Riggin has learned from her grandparents and great-grandparents the importance of sharing the gospel at every opportunity, even in the back seat of a car! The example of previous generations has been like seeds dropped in the fertile soil of Riggin's heart, bearing the fruit of a strong desire to pass the Baton of Truth to others.

My oldest daughter, Bell, has experienced much adversity in her friendships. She always takes a bold stand for the Lord and has been persecuted for it. Her friends don't seem to stick around for long. They can't handle being around someone who is strong in her convictions and cares more about doing the right thing than about being popular.

One night, before a particular friend group dropped her, she was able to share Christ with a girl who was interested in Christianity. Bell loves deeply and she loved this friend. She had been feeling compelled to share the gospel with this girl, and the conversation evolved naturally when the girl began to ask her questions about the Lord as they sat in their pj's at a friend's house at 2:00 a.m. The girl had been through a lot and seemed to soak up all that Bell shared with her. When Bell asked whether she would like to ask Jesus into her heart, the girl said yes. So, right there in that room in the middle of the night, Bell prayed with her to receive Christ!

Not long after, the same group of girls told Bell they no longer wanted to be friends with her because her faith in Jesus was too strong. We continue to pray for that girl, as the pressure so typical of teenage life today seems to be choking the budding faith inside her. Still, we know God placed Bell in that group for a season, all because He loved that girl so much and He knew Bell would faithfully lead her to Jesus.

God brought a friend named Grace into Sophia's life. Her name is doubly sweet now because we know God wanted His grace to permeate her life. She was at our house for the weekend, which was a welcome and common occurrence. She has been through much difficulty in her young life, and I'm so thankful that God brought her into our home so we could love on her. That Saturday morning, I got the girls up somewhat early to go to a store across town. As I began to drive, the Holy Spirit nudged me to share the gospel with her. Sophia had been planting seeds in her life for a long time, and I felt that God was letting me know it was harvesttime.

I shared with Grace my testimony and how I could never have survived some of the difficulties in my life if I hadn't had Jesus. I told her that He loves her, adores her, and has plans for her. When I looked in the rearview mirror, I saw tears streaming down her beautiful face. She said she had just received a hurtful phone call from a family member that morning, and it meant so much to hear that Jesus loves her. After we parked at the store, I asked whether Grace wanted to ask Jesus to come into her heart, forgive her sins, and be her heavenly Father. She said yes! With all of us crying, she repeated the prayer after me and became a sister in Christ. She was radiant and said she felt immediate peace. We continue to carry her in our hearts and on our knees in prayer. We praise God that He extended His grace to Grace. And to each of us.

My family has had the privilege of witnessing our parents and grandparents unashamedly sharing their faith with those around them. I pray that my girls and I will continue to follow in their footsteps and offer the same example to our children and grandchildren.

Never ever do I want to shrink back from sharing the gospel. I want to carry on the fire of previous generations for reaching the lost—and you can join me! If you didn't have that example in your home, you can become the witness the next generation needs. You and I don't have to be professionals. Just Jesus Followers who lead others to Him.

PHOTO BY MICHAEL GOMEZ

CREATING
A LEGACY OF WITNESS

*Every morning, ask God to open your eyes
to someone who needs Jesus today.*

Be a Jesus Follower: *Share the gospel.*

Go and make disciples of all nations.

Matthew 28:19

2

Popcorn and Chocolate Milk

While sharing the gospel with our words is a vital aspect of running the race, I've learned that our compassion and vulnerability also witness to the grace of God at work in our lives. I learned this from my mother's consistent presence through my difficult teen years.

My high school experience was miserable. From the outside, our public high school in downtown Raleigh was a spectacular historic stone structure, but to me it was a prison. To make matters worse, the big old building didn't have air-conditioning. North Carolina gets thick hot. That's how we describe air so hot and humid you could slice it up and serve it on a plate. This was especially true in early summer just before school let out and in late summer when school started. My homeroom was on the third floor facing downtown. Using toilet paper to wipe away the sweat pouring down her face, my homeroom teacher griped every morning that the "suits" downtown in their air-conditioned offices were the ones making the decision to keep us in school in inhumane heat. But the climate in the building wasn't the real misery; it was the fact that I was all alone in a school of 1,800 students.

In a way, my isolation was partially my choice. I've always been black and white in my walk with Jesus. Either you live for Him or you don't! During my midteens, that commitment left me on the fringes of high school society. The large number of friends I had going into high school quickly diminished because of peer pressure. I felt like I had become their conscience, and they either didn't want one or didn't want to be reminded that they had one. It wasn't that I told them how to live or condemned them for their choices. I just quietly chose not to go to parties or hang out with them when they were watching inappropriate movies. Shortly after I began to take that quiet stand, my friends started to turn their backs on me when I walked up to them in the halls at school. They stopped inviting me to do things with them. I was delighted one year to be invited to go to the beach with my friends for spring break, but wouldn't you know it? A week before the break, they disinvited me, saying the house was too full.

I used to beg my mom to write me a note to get out of going to school assemblies, because I had no one to sit with. When we had off-campus lunch, I sometimes drove to my dad's dental practice and ate my lunch in his office instead of going somewhere by myself.

My self-esteem was shot. Where I once was the life of the party, I now hardly said a word. But God in His infinite wisdom was working out His perfect plan. I realized at the time, praise God, that He was my best friend—He was the one I could talk to. I spent a lot of time in prayer before school and at night while I lay in bed, looking at the stars outside my window. He always knows what it will take to draw us to Himself. He gave me my life's verse while I was going through that difficult time, which is 1 Peter 4:12–13: "Dear friends, do not be surprised at the painful trial you are suffering, as though something strange were happening to you. But rejoice that you participate in the sufferings of Christ, so that you may be overjoyed when his glory is revealed." Eventually my heart absorbed the message. I wasn't a misfit. I was suffering for my faith in Jesus, and I shouldn't have been surprised. He had a purpose for this hardship, and He would be glorified through it!

As tough as things were, God knew how to bring some relief and peace, even while the storm was still raging. He did that through my mother. Every day after school, my mom met me at the door of our home. We'd walk into the kitchen, sit down at our big lazy Susan table, and have popcorn and chocolate milk. I can still picture how the sun hit the pine trees outside the kitchen window in the late afternoon. My mom would ask how my day had gone. And then, many times through tears, I would share the painful stories of the day. She'd listen and cry with me, pray with me, laugh with me, and just be with me. Those afternoons were priceless. Of course, in God's perfect plan, He had another purpose in those afternoon talks beyond my immediate need for comfort. He knew that one day I would be a mother of three girls who would face their own disappointments and challenges and be in need of God's love channeled through someone who understands.

Even though I may not remember all the words my mom spoke to me on those afternoons as we ate popcorn and drank chocolate milk, I'll never forget the comfort she brought me and the security I felt in being able to pour out my heart to her. She never belittled my situation or waved me off in exasperation after hearing some of the same heartaches over and over. She was patient in my affliction. She set an example that has inspired me to do the same with my girls. I've sacrificed sleep on countless nights just to sit on their beds while they pour out their hearts. I've cried with them because what hurts them hurts me too. I've counseled them, silently praying for wisdom. I've held them, shared Scripture with them, prayed with them, laughed with them, and dreamed with them.

While I don't know the specifics of your circumstances or whether you've been blessed by someone who sat with you in moments of pain, I am certain that your compassionate presence can be a witness to God's love for someone—perhaps a child, grandchild, niece, or nephew—who is hurting. When you talk with people who are experiencing difficulties, remember that Jesus is the ultimate example of a sympathetic presence that testifies of God's love. One of the scriptures I love to praise the Lord for is in Hebrews: "We do not have a High Priest who cannot sympathize with our weaknesses, but was in all points tempted as we are, yet without sin."[1] Jesus has been through it! He understands the suffering we are going through, because He has experienced it and handled it all without sin. What a comfort to know that Jesus understands! You and I should strive to be more like Him. Let's share our own hardships with others and let them know that we understand how difficult life can be. As we tell them how God brought us through something in the past or is carrying us through a challenge today, He will be glorified through the pain in our lives.

As witnesses to the grace of God, we can draw on the comfort we've received and encourage someone else going through something similar. Every situation we face has a purpose, whether we understand that purpose now or twenty years from now. He is trustworthy. He is reliable.

Now go share some popcorn and chocolate milk and a listening ear with someone who might need to tell you their story.

CREATING
A LEGACY OF WITNESS

What painful experiences in your life has God redeemed, and how can you comfort someone facing similar hardships?

Be a Jesus Follower: *Be a good listener.*

Praise be to the God and Father of our Lord Jesus Christ, the Father of compassion and the God of all comfort, who comforts us in all our troubles, so that we can comfort those in any trouble with the comfort we ourselves have received from God.

2 Corinthians 1:3–4

3

To Face Our Fears with Faith

As much as I want to emulate the bold witness of my parents and grandparents, I have had to lean into God's power to overcome my natural reticence and fear. I'm thankful for the role my mom has played in that process, deliberately giving me opportunities even as a child and teenager to pick up the Baton of Truth.

As I mentioned in the previous chapter, high school was hard for me in every way, and God in His mercy gave me multiple opportunities throughout my teens to travel with my mom. Each trip was unforgettable, but looking back on one particular travel experience when I was eighteen, I see that God was starting something in my life.

I fastened the straps securely over my chest as the pilot handed me earphones to drown out the noise of the rotor blades as they cut through the air. He climbed in beside me and began to push all kinds of buttons and levers in preparation for takeoff. My mom, who was no stranger to this adventure, sat behind me, relishing the chance to share this experience with me. I was focused on finding a motion sickness bag, wondering whether they even supplied those in the copilot's seat.

The pilot announced all was ready, and the helicopter lifted off, staying low to the ground, which only accentuated the sense of speed as we moved across the flat plain. As we sped above this expanse, the ground suddenly fell away. It felt as if the earth had dropped a mile down—and taken my stomach with it! There below us was the sparkling jewel of South Africa: Cape Town. Looking ahead, I saw the sun flickering off the ocean waves, like thousands of camera flashes in a stadium, while behind us the magnitude of Table Mountain was now visible. In the harbor below, huge ships were all lined up like fish anxiously awaiting feeding time. I could have jumped in there with them, because this was a feast for my eyes.

As captivated as I was by Cape Town's beauty, the real feast would be for my spirit after we were back on the ground. We were on this trip because my mom had been invited by a bishop in the Anglican church of South Africa, Frank Retief, and his wife, Beulah, to lead a conference at St. James Church in Cape Town. While she was busy preparing messages, I soaked in all the sights and savored the melodious South African accents, not realizing that God was about to open a door for me.

On the last day of the conference, my mom and the Reverend Retief asked whether I would be willing to give my testimony at the Sunday evening service. I had always been terrified of speaking in front of people. In fact, a speech class in high school almost paralyzed me with fear. At the start of the semester, the teacher had announced that, every day at the beginning of class, we would have to pick a slip of paper out of a bowl. On each slip was written a subject about which we would have to give a one-minute speech. One of the topics was to describe your first kiss. Having not yet had my first kiss, I was terrified to pick that slip of paper. My mom and I prayed for the whole year that I would never pick that topic, and I didn't!

As I considered the rector's invitation, I had to trust that the same faithful God who had held back the Red Sea for the Israelites and had held back that slip of paper for an entire school year would hold back my nerves that night in front of the congregation.

I remember thinking that there might be students in the audience who had a similar story and how encouraging it would be for them to know that they weren't alone. So I described what it had been like to be left out of conversations at school, to be ignored when walking down the halls, to notice classmates rolling their eyes as I walked to my car after school, and to spend each day counting down the minutes until school let out so I wouldn't have to hear everyone making plans for the weekend that didn't include me. I was alone because I had chosen not to compromise my walk with the Lord. I shared that, amid my loneliness at school, God had become my best friend.

My testimony that night wasn't anything spectacular, but I realize now that it was the beginning of God's call in my life. He is my Creator. He knows what gifts I have that may not be obvious, and with His gentle nudging, bit by bit, He has called me into a faith-filled adventure of witnessing to His goodness, whether on a platform or in my kitchen. Much like that helicopter ride, obeying His call can sometimes bring stomach-churning excitement. However, there are times when we have to obey God in the mundane situations we face every day at school, at work, or at home. Though I couldn't see it clearly at the time, I know God used my high school experience to focus my vision, exercise my gifts, and expand my usefulness for His glory.

I also learned the importance of trusting God in the face of fear and watching how He uses our difficulties for His own purposes and glory when we authentically give witness to Him.

Exactly one week after my mom and I spoke at that service in Cape Town, four terrorists stormed into St. James Church, shooting automatic rifles and lobbing hand grenades into that same Sunday evening service where we had spoken the week before. Eleven people were killed, and fifty-eight were injured. I was shaken to my core that this vibrant congregation had been so brutally attacked. I was also keenly aware that God had chosen to spare my mom and me. In the following days, God used that event to put a national spotlight on the people in that church. They came together in front of the world and forgave the attackers. South Africa was in the middle of dismantling apartheid, and God used that horrific event to showcase forgiveness in the face of tremendous suffering. Subsequently the entire nation heard the gospel, with hundreds of people giving their lives to Jesus Christ.

I'm reminded that God has a plan for every part of our lives—every event, every moment of every day. I'm learning to trust His never-ending, all-encompassing faithfulness as I follow Him in obedience no matter what I'm facing. He knows the way I am to take. He has promised to lead me in right paths. And it's this steadfast trust in His leadership—in Him—through the ups and downs, the hard places and the good, that I want to pass on to my children.

Just as my mom urged me, I want to urge my girls to step out and bear witness to their faith, even if it seems as scary as the ground falling away on a helicopter ride, because then they will receive the blessing of experiencing His faithfulness firsthand.

Won't you join us by trusting God to use your story for His glory?

CREATING
A LEGACY OF WITNESS

*What frightening situation has God brought you
through so that you can be a witness to the next
generation of His faithfulness and goodness?*

Be a Jesus Follower: *Share your testimony.*

When the Counselor comes, whom I will send
to you from the Father, the Spirit of truth who
goes out from the Father, he will testify about me;
but you also must testify.

John 15:26–27

4

Running into Grace

A common misconception about my family is that since both of my grandfathers were evangelists and preachers, everyone in the family must be saints. In reality, we are all a bunch of sinners, making mistakes, in need of discipline and correction. The fact that you and I are fallible humans provides opportunities to be witnesses to God's grace, if we only listen to His leading.

When my mom was growing up and even when I was growing up, kids were allowed a lot more freedom than most have today. The freedom was good for developing magnificent imaginations but not so good when we were left to our own devices. Sometimes that led to bad decisions and tough consequences.

We grew up hearing stories about how, when being disciplined, my mom and her siblings would crawl out the windows of their locked rooms, step onto the roof, and climb over the top of the house in order to enter another sibling's room; or how my Aunt Gigi slammed the courtyard door on my Uncle Franklin, cutting off the top of one of his fingers; or how one of my mom's sisters forced her to go door to door in the autumn, selling colored leaves to neighbors who had yards full of colored leaves; or how that sister hid behind a tree stump and threw mud balls at passing cars, then pushed my mom out to take the blame when the driver stopped the car and pronounced judgment.

I'm not sure our childhood fights ever reached the level of the epic battles that my mom had with her siblings, but we may have managed to come in a close second. I'm ashamed to say that my sister and I could get pretty ugly at times.

One afternoon Morrow and I had gotten into yet another knock-down, drag-out fight. Usually when one of us did something to upset the other, we would draw an invisible line down the middle of the bedroom we shared and forbid the other person to cross it—or else. The "or else" usually involved throwing things or hitting each other. Really mature stuff. Unfortunately on this particular afternoon, I did something to push Morrow beyond the limits of her patience. She chased me out of our room, down the stairs, through the kitchen, and around the corner toward the back door.

Running for my life, I felt my heart pounding, my adrenaline pumping, and terror spurring me on. Still, Morrow was closing in fast. My memory of the scene is all in slow motion. As I rounded the corner, I could see the glass door ahead barring my way to freedom. I opened the latch as fast as I could, and in my adrenaline-fueled panic, I slammed it right as she reached me. What I hadn't anticipated in that moment of victory was that the glass would shatter on impact. Into a million shards. Much to my shame, I didn't even turn around to look. I knew I was as good as dead.

My mom and dad were so authoritative that George Washington, Napoleon, and General Patton all would have stood at attention and saluted if they ever heard their names called by either one. We always teased my mom that she had one particular look with the power to stop us as abruptly as if a pack of wolves had jumped in our path, making our insides go numb. My dad didn't take the time to even give us a look. He would whip out his belt and snap it in his hands before we could blink. While my parents certainly never abused us, they did execute judgment at appropriate times.

In the wake of the shattering glass, I didn't pause to catch a look, hear my name, or listen for the sound of leather. My sense of guilt and the certainty of the dire consequences to come sent me running to the best hiding spot I could think of: the back-seat floorboard of my mom's navy-blue station wagon. I roasted in the close confines of the stifling car. But I really started to sweat when I heard Mom calling me. Chills snaked up my spine, as if I were playing in some horror version of hide-and-seek.

My mom came into the garage, yelling my name. Eight years of obedience training had taught me to respond when being called. I knew I had stalled long enough. I opened the door of the car and climbed out, my face on fire from embarrassment and shame. My mom said in a booming voice, "Go to your room!" If she said anything else, I didn't hear it over the locomotive roar of blood rushing through my veins.

My parents must have known that solitude would give me time to think about my actions. I felt horrible as I wondered whether Morrow had gotten hurt. I also felt horrible as I wondered about the pain to be inflicted on my backside. I contemplated packing my pants with stuffed animals to cushion the sting of the spankings that were sure to come. As if my dad wouldn't notice the shape of Peter Rabbit under my sweatpants!

Then I heard the familiar creak of our stairs, and I knew my dad was coming. I braced myself for the look of disappointment and the inevitable consequences. Dad came in and sat down on the edge of my bed, causing the springs to squeak. I remember the lights weren't on, but the late-afternoon sun cast shadows across the room.

What happened next took me completely by surprise. "Rach, I want to teach you about grace," my dad said. "What you did was wrong. You deserve to be punished and spanked." (He even gritted his teeth dramatically when he said it.) "But instead of punishing you for breaking the glass door, I am going to take you to get ice cream."

I felt like time had frozen while my brain processed what I was hearing. I began to cry. Dad went on to explain that his grace to me was a picture of God's grace to us. We deserve death for our sins, but God sent His Son to the cross to take away our sins and give us eternal life.

When we place our faith in Him, we no longer live under the horror of knowing our sins are sending us to hell. Instead, because of His grace, we are forgiven and blessed, and we can walk in freedom.

I think that was the first time I truly grasped what grace is, and I've never forgotten it. So many times people run from God, like I ran from my parents. We want to hide because we know we are guilty. We are ashamed and afraid of the punishment that we surely deserve. The magnificent thing that no human brain can ever fully grasp is how deep and wide is God's love for us. He knows where we are hiding and why we are hiding. Yet He comes to us, wraps His arms around us, and extends His grace to us, covering our sin with His blood. He wipes away our sin—forever! His Word says so.

Before you can teach your children, grandchildren, or others to run to God, you need to run to Him yourself. When you do, you will find a loving heavenly Father who extends His grace to you. Once you've received His love and grace, it will be your joy and privilege to freely extend them to others.

CREATING
A LEGACY OF WITNESS

What ungodly actions, words, or attitudes do you need to confess to God so that you can receive His forgiveness and walk in freedom?

Be a Jesus Follower: *Extend grace.*

I will forgive their wickedness and will remember their sins no more.

Hebrews 8:12

Freely you have received, freely give.

Matthew 10:8

5

Hidden Treasures

One of the ways we give witness to the truth of the gospel is simply by reflecting God's perspective and priorities in our daily lives and letting Him shine through our distinct personalities.

My grandmother Tai Tai always knew how to stretch a dollar. She grew up on the mission field in China, where she and her family had to learn how to be thrifty and creative because they didn't have much in the way of material things. As an eighteen-year-old girl, Tai Tai made the long trip from China to America on an ocean liner by herself in order to attend Wheaton College. I can't imagine how hard it must have been to leave her family and all she had ever known to come to a new place and attend college with a bunch of students who had grown up in a totally different culture. She didn't arrive on campus with loads of suitcases and bags, as I'm sure many of the others did. Other than a few basic skirts and blouses appropriate for attending classes, the only dress Tai Tai owned was a simple black one.

I asked her once how she did it. How did she avoid feeling insecure about her seemingly inadequate wardrobe? As she answered

my question, the sweet expression on her face showed no bitterness or resentfulness—a witness, in and of itself, to the peace she
felt about it.

As she shared with me her memories of that season, she smiled
and wistfully explained that even though she had only one dress, she
owned several scarves that she would tie around her neck to make
the dress feel like a different outfit every time she wore it. And for
special occasions, she added a single strand of imitation pearls.

With that one black dress, she ended up catching the eye of, dating, and then marrying the greatest evangelist since the apostle Paul!
Her wardrobe certainly wasn't what drew my grandfather to her. It
was her character and the presence of the Lord on her bright face
that captured his attention.

Maybe that very experience of having only one black dress in college is what nurtured Tai Tai's creativity and eye for seeing beyond
the superficial value of things to their true potential. I am sure Daddy
Bill appreciated Tai Tai's keen ability to spot and bring to life the discarded or unnoticed. He got a front-row seat to it for sixty-five years.
The Lord knew she would need that creativity as they started their
life together with only a few resources. When she and Daddy Bill got
married, Tai Tai made her own wedding dress, a simple yet elegant
fitted satin dress with a scoop neck and long sleeves. She kept her
wedding dress stored for all those years, and on their sixtieth wedding anniversary, Tai Tai was able to put it back on to surprise Daddy
Bill. It had withstood the test of time, as had her stunning figure and
their beautiful marriage.

Tai Tai also knew how to repurpose things, creating beautiful items
with a little bit of money and a lot of vision. When her first baby was
born, she used her gorgeous wedding veil to decorate the bassinet that
each of her children would sleep in for his or her first several weeks
of life. That bassinet has cradled three generations of Graham babies:
my mom and her siblings, me and my siblings, and my three girls.
However, by the time it got to my girls, my mom had to use that same
creative gene when she took off Tai Tai's well-worn wedding veil and

replaced it with my wedding veil. It was so meaningful to have each of my girls sleep in the same spot where so many members of my family had started their lives.

Tai Tai had an impressive talent for turning something ordinary into something wonderful. When they were building their home up on the mountain, Daddy Bill was traveling and speaking, so Tai Tai did what she could to put together a big log cabin that, to me, looked like it had a hint of old-town Williamsburg with a dose of English cottage. In order to do that, she had to be thrifty and think outside the box.

She scoured the area and found old bricks in Asheville. Some of those bricks were handmade and stamped with *Biltmore* (from the village outside the historic Biltmore Estate). The wood used to build the house came from a collection of old log cabins. She personally salvaged the old wooden beams, planks, and panels as well as some spectacular hand-hewn logs. When she lacked all the beams she needed, she had the carpenter mill some from new lumber. They didn't look worn and old enough for her liking, she told me, so she rubbed each beam with shoe polish and lipstick until she got the look she wanted.

She found an old door that she wanted to use for the front hall closet. When she showed it to the carpenter, he exclaimed, "A man can't take no pride in this kind of work!" Rumor is that he quit because he was so disgusted to work with something he considered junk. But to Tai Tai, every aspect of their unorthodox cabin was charming. Little did he know what a beloved and homey gathering place it would become.

Another of my grandmother's money-saving home-design secrets was to handcraft their light fixtures. When initially installed, the ceiling lights were just bare bulbs. To make them look less plain, Tai Tai covered some of the light bulbs with a variety of mason jars and woven baskets. Even after she went to Heaven, one of her original makeshift basket light fixtures still hung in what had once been my Uncle Ned's upstairs bedroom. How many nights had I sat up in that very bedroom, reading or thinking next to the warm glow of that light.

Tai Tai was never idle. I think her mind was in overdrive with endless ideas all day, every day. I remember once walking into her kitchen and finding her on all fours, drawing on a braided rag rug. When I asked what she was doing, she said that she didn't think the rug had enough blue on it so she'd decided to use a blue Sharpie on some of the braids.

We all loved her mountain cabin, which was permeated with her touch, but not everyone who came to visit appreciated its unique qualities. She shared with me that when Muhammad Ali came, he had intended to spend the night in the guest room. He was expecting a gorgeous mansion, but when he arrived and saw how rustic it was, he asked to stay in a hotel, much to Tai Tai's amusement.

Tai Tai was creative and confident and thrifty and never let the world and all its frippery change her. Once, she and Daddy Bill were asked to attend a formal dinner with elite dignitaries, but she didn't have anything to wear and had no time to go shopping. In typical Tai Tai fashion, she looked through the clothing in her luggage to see whether she could turn anything into something formal. That evening she attended the formal dinner in her nightgown, dressed up with a string of pearls! I know she must have looked amazingly elegant.

Her eye for the discarded helped us out when Steven and I were just a young couple, trying to decorate our home on a tight budget. We were so excited to finally be settling down after a bit of uncertainty as to where the Lord would have us live. Like most newly married couples, we had only a little bit of money, definitely not enough for new furniture. My parents and in-laws kindly offered us a few old pieces of furniture from their homes. But the most special piece came from my grandmother's house—and it wasn't even furniture at first.

One of the best parts of living in North Carolina was that we were so close to my grandparents' house—only a three-and-half-hour drive from their doorstep in the mountains. Shortly after moving into our new little house, we drove up to visit Tai Tai for a weekend. She asked us all about our new house. As we sat and talked, she got a gleam in her eye that suggested she was formulating a plan. She put the tips of her fingers together as she so often did when she was thinking, then told us to go to the old cabin used for storage on her mountain property and get the old molasses shaker we'd find there. Her idea was to have Steven turn it into a bookcase.

We headed down the long winding driveway toward the cabin, hoping that we'd be able to spot what she was talking about, since neither of us knew what a molasses shaker looked like. We entered the old cabin, looking out for the snakes and flying squirrels known to use that cabin as their own mountain motel. As we rummaged through random pieces of wood, old chairs, and discarded tables, being mindful of splinters and rusty nails, we finally found what Tai Tai had described. The molasses shaker looked like a six-foot-long, two-and-a-half-foot-wide trough with wooden sides and a metal belly. Wooden handles stuck out of the four corners, where people apparently would hold the long trough over a fire and cook molasses.

Tai Tai was delighted that we had found it. She sketched on a piece of paper how Steven could turn the old molasses shaker into a bookshelf. Armed with her idea and the molasses shaker, we drove home, and Steven went to work on putting it together. It worked! We called Tai Tai to tell her how it turned out, and she was "tickled to death," as she would say.

To this day, that bookshelf stands proudly in our house. Even though it cost us only a few dollars to fix up, it is priceless to me.

Tai Tai never forgot the lessons she learned growing up on the mission field. She saw value in things that no one else would notice. In fact, years ago she spotted an old table upside down in a chicken coop and immediately had the vision to see it transformed into an elegant dining table. She encouraged my mom to buy it, and it has since hosted at least a thousand dinners in my mom's dining room. Yes, Tai Tai had an eye for beauty even if it had chicken droppings all over it.

Tai Tai didn't just see the hidden treasures in odds and ends, but she recognized the hidden treasure in people too. I was one of those people. I have always struggled with low self-esteem. As a teenager, I hated looking in the mirror because I would see my curly, frizzy hair. I grew to my full height of over five feet, eleven inches in eighth grade, making me feel awkward around kids my age who were almost all shorter than me. I felt like I didn't have the striking beauty of my sister, and I didn't attract the attention of boys the way she seemed to. I shed many tears on my pillow at night. With a loving grandmother's intuition, Tai Tai took notice of the pain in my heart. She wrote me letters encouraging me and speaking life into me, letters that I have kept as the treasures they are. The following paragraph is from one such letter:

> *I want you to know that I recognize true beauty when I see it. Not in beauty pageants, or highly paid models, or on magazine covers. God is developing His own beauties through pain, disappointment, humiliation, trials of every kind . . . and the one who clings to the Lord with determination, God makes beautiful.*

I wonder whether you, too, have struggled with something about yourself that you can't seem to change. Your hair. Your height. Your weight. The color of your eyes or skin. Just as Tai Tai stated so beautifully, you and I have a heavenly Father who looks inside us and sees beauty and strength and value. He isn't looking at the outward appearance or at the bazillion mistakes we've made. He doesn't listen to our negative thoughts or the countless insecurities that we berate ourselves over. Instead, He takes all that we are—our mess, our inadequacies, and our rough exterior and interior—and He masterfully turns it into something of great value.

If only I could wake up every morning and remember this when "the accuser of [the] brethren"[1] whispers to me that I am worthless. It is easy to entertain thoughts of insignificance or inadequacy that make us feel like discarded trash, much like that rusty molasses shaker looked to me. But we have a heavenly Father who is able to redeem our shortcomings, create beauty from what others see as flawed, and give us the abundance of His presence and peace in the midst of deprivation.

Just as Tai Tai saw and called forth the hidden treasure in me, I want to see that in my girls, as well as in other people. If we see people as God sees them, our witness will be more winsome and inviting. Imagine how much brighter our days will be if we choose to view ourselves and others the way Tai Tai viewed practically everything: as a priceless hidden treasure!

Happy hunting!

CREATING
A LEGACY OF WITNESS

Every morning, ask God to help you see each person around you the way He sees him or her: as a beautiful treasure of inestimable worth.

Be a Jesus Follower: *See with His eyes.*

The LORD said to Samuel, "Do not consider his appearance or his height, for I have rejected him. The LORD does not look at the things man looks at. Man looks at the outward appearance, but the LORD looks at the heart."

1 Samuel 16:7

6

A Reflection of God's Faithful Love

I come from a long line of women who are opinionated, witty, and strong willed—not exactly the submissive type. These qualities don't usually bode well for a healthy marriage, unless Jesus is at the center of it.

Marriage is a lifelong commitment, no matter how desperately you and I may want to kick our spouses to the curb on occasion. Even more important than producing godly offspring, the goal in marriage is to reflect God's love relationship with us.[1] While some people, such as my own brother and sister, may not have children, they can still be fruitful with spiritual offspring.[2] And your faithful devotion to your spouse, no matter how hard it gets, is a witness to the world of God's faithfulness.

I've often thought that God uses two different kinds of marriages to mold us: the first is where the husband and wife are stronger together because of the love they share, and the second is where God uses the difficulty of being together to draw each of them closer to Him. Both kinds of marriage can glorify the Lord, but if you allow it, I think the difficult marriage offers more opportunities to cultivate a more intimate relationship with Jesus where you rely on Him instead of a spouse to meet your needs. However, if we don't value those marriage challenges as a way for God's grace to shine through, we will fail in giving our children, grandchildren, and the world around us a clear witness to God's sustaining love and presence.

Tai Tai and Daddy Bill had the first kind of marriage, the kind where they were so in love with each other that they were stronger because of it. They beautifully reflected the relationship we are to have with Jesus. They managed to stay deeply in love despite the pressures of living in a fishbowl and the difficulty of weeks and even months of separation because of Daddy Bill's travels.

How did they do it? More specifically, how did my grandmother not only remain in the marriage but also maintain a vibrant love relationship with Daddy Bill for almost sixty-four years?

Daddy Bill's absences were often at critical times. He missed the births of most of his five children. On one occasion, after being gone for many months during the Los Angeles tent revival that launched much of his international ministry, an eighteen-month-old baby toddled into his hotel room. He looked at her, then asked, "Who is this?" He did not recognize the toddler—my mother—as his own daughter! His preaching responsibilities also kept him from attending the funeral of his mother-in-law, Tai Tai's beloved mother. Why did these absences not cause deep bitterness in Tai Tai?

Because of Daddy Bill's extended absences, Tai Tai operated as a single parent. Not only was she the sole disciplinarian for a slew of strong-willed children; she was also the one who tucked them into bed, read them bedtime stories, helped with their homework, met with irate schoolteachers . . . and the list goes on and on. She was not a single parent, so why did she have to function like one? Why wasn't she filled with resentment and bitterness?

Why did she never complain or accuse Daddy Bill of leaving her at the very times when she may have needed him the most? Why didn't she hold him back from his calling . . . or at least urge him to cut back?

With my sin nature, I'm sure I would have drop-kicked him out the door on multiple occasions. I remember asking Tai Tai, "How did you do it? How did you manage to not only stay married but grow in your love for him, accept him and his call to preach, yet never become bitter?"

Her answer at that time was to laugh and say, with sparkling eyes that flashed with mischievous energy, that the secret to her legendarily happy marriage was his frequent absences!

While I laughed at the time, I knew there was much more depth to her experience than what she was saying. I saw the depth in the worn pages of her Bible. I saw it in the big black notebooks on the shelf beside her bed that held Psalms printed in letters over an inch high so that she could continue reading even after her vision deteriorated because of macular degeneration. I heard it in her voice when she prayed. I saw it in the light that radiated from her face when she talked about Jesus . . . or Daddy Bill. I knew that a strong undercurrent had carried her through a marriage that wasn't easy.

The undercurrent that was present in Tai Tai's life—the same undercurrent that I deeply desire to flow through my life and into the lives of my girls—was a vibrant, personal love relationship with Jesus, developed through prayer and Bible reading. A legacy that was passed on to my mom in abundance.

My mom's childhood bedroom was located above Tai Tai's room, and they both enjoyed beautiful views of the mountain ridge east of the house. My mother remembers seeing light pour out of Tai Tai's window onto the trees of the mountainside late at night or before the sun rose. She knew Tai Tai was either on her knees in prayer or bent over one of her many translations of Scripture, filling her heart and mind with God's Word, because that's exactly the way my mom would find her when she slipped down the back staircase and entered Tai Tai's room.

If you were to open one of Tai Tai's Bibles, you would find notes and highlights and pages worn from use. Her Bible was her treasure! She knew that within it lay all the riches life could offer—riches that last. I can still picture her long, elegant fingers holding her Bible with such reverence. She clung to it. She knew that through the Holy Scriptures she would find comfort when she was lonely, strength when she had none, peace when worries assailed her, answers when questions came to mind, and hope for the life yet to come. I can say with full confidence that if someone were to ask about her favorite possession—was it a gift from the Queen of England, one of the rare books that she so loved to collect, or a piece of lace from June Carter Cash?—without hesitation she would have said it was her Bible.

Studying her Bible is what gave my grandmother the wisdom to handle every situation, such as when she welcomed Daddy Bill home from a long absence with great fanfare and honored him in front of her children. When he left on a trip, she didn't fuss or nag or make a big deal about it, especially not in front of her kids. One of her famous quips was that she was determined to "make the least of all that goes and the most of all that comes." She embraced his calling and gave him her full support. She prayed for him faithfully, so much so that she had calluses on her knees.

Bitterness could have easily crept in. But it never did. She chose not to allow it to take root. She chose to honor her husband. She chose to support him in his calling. She chose to let him go. I've found out for myself how hard it is to let go of what I want. But when I do, God amazingly fulfills each need—more than a husband ever could. When Tai Tai told me with a twinkle in her eye that the time she and Daddy Bill spent apart helped their marriage, I believe that was true because she made the choice to allow the absences to be a positive experience rather than a negative one.

After almost a lifetime of traveling, Daddy Bill came home and spent those last precious years with Tai Tai by her bedside. The miracle is that she welcomed him home. No bitterness, no record of wrongs, no resentment. She simply held his hand and gazed at him with eyes so intimately in love that you would feel as if you'd intruded on a private moment even amid casual conversation. I saw firsthand unconditional love that reflected Christ's love for us.

Tai Tai submitted her strong will to God, giving voice to her opinionated spirit and passion through her poems. And she defused tension and negative situations with a rollicking sense of humor. We all dearly loved her wit. Praise the Lord for Tai Tai's surrendered life to Christ. She chose to follow Christ daily in her marriage by studying Scripture and praying to the God who hears and sees.

I wonder whether you might be comparing this love story—this beautiful witness to what God can accomplish—with your own situation. Are you in a difficult marriage? Is your spouse absent a lot, perhaps traveling with work or fighting for our country overseas while you raise the kids? Did your husband miss the birth of your child? Has your spouse wronged you in some way and you can't let it go? Does he not know how to comfort your grieving heart after the loss of a loved one? Does he not voice the same hurt you feel over your wayward teenager?

To be honest, even with our shared passion for serving Jesus, married life is at times really hard for me. My husband is a coach and therefore gone for most of the year, but my challenges aren't about wanting more attention from Steven. I was a tomboy growing up, and I am still independent and strong. My struggle has been trying to mesh two totally different personalities.

I have learned firsthand as well as from Tai Tai's witness that the only answer to a tough marriage—or any marriage—is Jesus Christ and His Word. I have crumpled to the floor in tears over my marriage at times, desperate for wisdom from Jesus. And through His Word, He becomes my comfort. Through His Word, He becomes my encourager. Through His Word, He fills my heart with love for Steven and for Himself.

But before I even open up His Word, I have to tell Jesus I'm sorry. I have to acknowledge my sins. Whether it was yelling at Steven, saying something hurtful to him, accusing him of something in an angry way, or any one of the myriad other offenses I have committed. After I've sincerely confessed my sins to the Lord, naming each one, then and only then am I able to hear God's voice through His Word.

I've found that naming my sins, one by one, before a holy and righteous King is personally humiliating but spiritually refreshing. The Lord already knows our sins, but when we confess them, He knows that we know that He knows.

So, dear reader, be encouraged. When you and I confess and repent, turning away from bitterness, turning away from anger, turning away from unforgiveness, then we can rest in the loving arms of Jesus and let Him be our Sustainer and the Lifter of our heads.[3]

You may be thinking, *Well, that's great, but what about the husband who is mostly at fault?* God's Word says that love "keeps no record of wrongs."[4] God has given me several godly examples of this, lived out in the flesh. My grandmother beautifully portrayed that sacrificial love. However, in writing this, I recognize the grievous reality that some wives face abuse by their husbands. If you are experiencing abuse, I gently encourage you to seek help from trustworthy sources.

My husband and I have gone through some dark times, times when I didn't think I could take one more hour, let alone a lifetime of marriage. But as I've looked to God and to the examples He's given me in my parents and grandparents, I've made it through those tough times. God is faithful and will always see us through. If our marriages are to reflect Jesus, then we will be slow to speak and quick to listen, quick to forgive, overflowing with grace, clothed with humility, keeping no record of wrongs, and filled with unconditional love. It's a tall order, but the Holy Spirit gives us all that we need for a successful marriage. The choice is ours.

Look at sweet Tai Tai. She did it! And I am so glad that she did. Her family of five children, nineteen grandchildren, and over forty great-grandchildren—as well as the entire world through her support of Daddy Bill's ministry—has been affected by her ability through Christ to let go and love unconditionally.

PHOTO BY RUSS BUSBY

CREATING
A LEGACY OF WITNESS

*Whether in your marriage or in another relationship,
what frustration, bitterness, or unmet expectation
do you need to ask God to help you surrender?*

Be a Jesus Follower: *Don't hold back, hold on,
or hold out. Give God everything.*

Love must be sincere. . . . Be devoted to one
another in brotherly love. Honor one another
above yourselves.

Romans 12:9–10

7

Embracing the Fullness
of God's Family

In June 1995, Daddy Bill was in Toronto, getting ready to hold one of his crusades. Amid a flurry of media interviews and appearances for several days preceding the crusade, he began to feel really sick. He eventually collapsed and was rushed to the hospital, where the doctors discovered that he had a bleeding colon.

I remember my mom quickly leaving Raleigh to fly up to be with him as he spent five days in the hospital. Of course, someone had to fill in for him at his crusade. It was a big deal because he always preached at his crusades. Whom would Daddy Bill trust to fill the pulpit on such short notice?

Ralph Bell was the man Daddy Bill turned to. Dr. Bell had joined the Billy Graham Evangelistic Association as an associate evangelist in 1965, the second African American to do so. He held mini crusades all over the world and was a gifted preacher. Daddy Bill called on him to fill in at the Toronto crusade, knowing he could trust this friend and ministry partner to teach God's Word with power, passion, and accuracy. Daddy Bill loved Dr. Bell's heart for the gospel and his desire to see lives changed by it.

I never saw Daddy Bill treat anyone with disrespect because of his or her race, religion, or background. His heart was to share the gospel with as many people as possible. Even amid the era of segregation, he opened up his crusades to everyone, going so far as to personally cut down the ropes meant to separate his crusade audience by the color of their skin.

I'm so thankful for Daddy Bill's example of loving and accepting all people, and I'm deeply grateful my other grandparents did the same. My Grampa Lotz pastored a predominately African American and Hispanic congregation on the Grand Concourse in the Bronx. Gramma was the only white woman in the choir. I remember visiting as a child and being loved on by all the members of his church. At Grampa's funeral, half the church was filled with African American people coming to honor him.

My parents also reflected in their every interaction the truth that "God so loved the world."[1] Most weekends while I was growing up, our house was filled with athletes from the University of North Carolina and from North Carolina State University. All were warmly welcomed without regard for what color their skin was. Dad just wanted some good competition on the basketball half court in our backyard. My mom cooked for them and made homemade ice cream. Although my dad drew athletes to the house through their love for playing ball, his heart was to disciple those young men to be godly leaders. One in particular, Carey Casey, has had a huge impact on all of us. He was a running back from the famous high school football team portrayed in the movie *Remember the Titans*. He went on to play at UNC, where he met my dad, who was leading their Fellowship of Christian Athletes huddle.

One of the regulars at our house, Carey was always filled with more joy than almost anyone else I have ever met. If my dad had been asked about his favorite people of all time, Carey would be at the top of the list. Daddy Bill believed so firmly in Carey's potential that he paid for Carey's tuition at Gordon-Conwell Theological Seminary. And it's clear their respect for Carey was well placed. He has spent much of his adult life ministering to inner-city kids in Chicago. His passion is to equip fathers to be godly influences in the home. He speaks all over the country, has been the chaplain for the Dallas Cowboys and the Kansas City

Chiefs, was a part of the White House Task Force for Fatherhood and Healthy Families, and is a pastor in the inner city of Chicago. He credits my dad with being an enormous influence on his life.

About a year after my dad passed away, Carey came to visit our family. He wanted to check on my mom and make sure she was okay. He spoke to my girls as a father would, challenging them to love the Lord and grow in their relationship with Him. And then Carey put his hands on my girls' heads and prayed a father's blessing over them. We were all crying. Each time we are with him and his wife, Melanie, we are beyond blessed and lifted in our spirits. He exemplifies a Christ-filled life.

Another man who often came into our home when I was young was Nicky Cruz, a former New York City gang leader. Nicky was born in Puerto Rico to a father who was a satanic priest and a mother who was a witch doctor. They beat Nicky on multiple occasions to within inches of his life. They cursed the day he was born. They wanted nothing to do with him. So, at a young age, he was out on his own. He ended up in New York City as a leader of one of the worst gangs at that time. He was filled with rage and bitterness and hatred. He committed many crimes and was in and out of jail.

One day, a young preacher by the name of David Wilkerson invited Nicky and his gang, as well as other gangs, to come hear him preach. They decided to come to fight one another, with no intention of listening to the skinny preacher. When Nicky heard him preaching, he walked straight up to him and punched him several times and spit on him. But David looked right at him and said, "Nicky, Jesus loves you!" Nicky later said that, for the next two weeks, no matter where he was—sleeping with his girlfriend, robbing somebody, stabbing somebody—all he could hear was "Nicky, Jesus loves you!" Shortly after, he went forward at another service where David was preaching and gave his heart to Jesus. He said all the anger left him immediately.

God radically changed his life, and Nicky has now preached to millions of people all over the world, sharing the gospel of Jesus Christ and telling them how much Jesus loves them. My dad took me to Daddy Bill's crusade in Central Park my senior year in high school. At that crusade,

Nicky Cruz shared his testimony with the hundreds of thousands who came, in the very place where he had once fought in gang wars.

Nicky, his wife, and his daughters lived in Raleigh for several years, which gave us the blessing of getting to know them. I remember him teaching my brother how to protect himself after he had been beaten up by six upperclassmen in the stairwell at his high school. Even though I knew him as a young girl, Nicky's impact is still felt in my life today as I observe how he continues to faithfully preach the gospel of Jesus Christ that changed his life so many years ago.

As an adult, I went to Times Square Church to hear David Wilkerson, the pastor who had led Nicky Cruz to faith in Jesus. I cried sitting there, just thinking about what a bold man of God he was. So many years after leading Nicky Cruz to Christ, he was still just as passionate about saving the lost.

As I think of others who have inspired me and my family, I picture R. V. Brown, who has the biggest triceps I have ever seen in my life! This dear black evangelist also has a deep, rich voice and the fire of Elijah. Like me, his faith was nurtured by a family determined to pass on the Baton of Truth. He grew up as one of seventeen brothers and sisters with parents who loved the Lord. He witnesses to literally everyone he comes in contact with. He leads people to Christ in the middle of weight rooms, in restaurants, on planes, in parking lots—anywhere.

We met RV through the Fellowship of Christian Athletes. He was the chaplain for the Tampa Bay Buccaneers for years. He frequently speaks to football teams around the country. Whenever he speaks, everyone in the room hangs on every word he says. He is an evangelist through and through. Recently my husband, Steven, invited RV to speak to his football team. When RV gave the invitation to receive Christ as Savior, almost the entire team went forward for prayer! He has prayed for my girls, encouraged my mom by leaving powerful prayers on her answering machine, and spent hours talking with my dad on multiple occasions. And no matter what he is doing or whom he is with, he talks about the Lord with his every breath.

My grandparents and parents have given me an example of loving all people and learning from fellow believers no matter their race or background, and I desire to do the same for my girls. We have been members of a predominately African American church for most of my adult life. When I was in school at Baylor University, I drove ninety minutes one way in order to sit under the teaching of Tony Evans, pastor of Oak Cliff Bible Fellowship. I'm not sure anyone—black, white, Hispanic, or Asian—can match Dr. Evans for the passionate clarity of his biblical exposition.

But Peter Rochelle, who pastors Church on the Rock in Raleigh, is a close second. He is an expository preacher who loves God's Word and speaks with conviction and passion week after week. There is never a Sunday when I walk away without having been convicted, challenged, or encouraged by something. I am so thankful for his godly influence on my girls through his excellent teaching.

Each of these men has shown me what godly leadership looks like. They have shown me what a vibrant relationship with Jesus looks like. They have shown me what compassionate and urgent evangelism looks like. They have simply shown me what the genuine love of Jesus looks like, a love that embraces people of every skin color, economic background, and culture. I am only one of thousands of people whom they have influenced, but I have taken note of their example, and I pray that I can carry on that Baton of Truth in my witness.

If you and I intend to bear witness to God's character and truth, we need to seek out trustworthy voices who will challenge and encourage us and our families in our spiritual growth. What's more, we need people speaking into our lives from a wide variety of backgrounds and ethnicities so that we reflect the beauty of God's love in the diversity of our relationships. Remember, God told the prophet Samuel that He does not look at the outward appearance but instead looks at the heart.[2] Racism, prejudice, and discrimination are from the pit of hell and have no place in the hearts of believers in Jesus. Heaven will be filled with every tribe and every tongue. Shouldn't our homes and our churches reflect our heavenly Home? I'm so thankful that those who nurtured my faith believed this. My life is immeasurably richer because of it.

CREATING A LEGACY OF WITNESS

Today ask God to free you from any misconceptions or prejudices that may be holding you back from fellowshipping fully with someone of another ethnicity or culture.

Be a Jesus Follower: *Love all God's children.*

You are worthy to take the scroll and to open its seals, because you were slain, and with your blood you purchased men for God from every tribe and language and people and nation. You have made them to be a kingdom and priests to serve our God, and they will reign on the earth.

Revelation 5:9–10

PART TWO

Our Worship

Seth also had a son, and he named him Enosh. At that time men began to call on the name of the LORD.

Genesis 4:26

An authentic witness is inextricably linked to a heart devoted to worship. As we've seen, Abel effectively passed the Baton of Truth to his little brother, Seth, who then passed it to his son Enosh. It was during Enosh's lifetime that people began to call on the name of the Lord. The subtle implication is that Enosh in some way helped lead people in worship.

The Motivation for Worship

What would have motivated Enosh to worship God? I wonder whether it was the negative example of his Uncle Cain, who would still have been alive in Enosh's lifetime. Did Enosh see the misery of his uncle, who lived with not only a guilty conscience but also the consequences of his sin? Did he see Cain's obvious restlessness as he wandered from place to place, unable to settle down in peace? Did he see the bitterness that had taken root in society, destroying everything that was noble and kind and decent and good so that the civilization of his day was increasingly wicked?[1]

Has someone served as a negative example for you? Do you have an "Uncle Cain," someone who has rebelled against God and is living an interesting life but has no real peace or joy or lasting satisfaction? Such an example can be a powerful motivation to make real worship a priority in your life.

While Enosh witnessed the negative example of his Uncle Cain, he also was given a front-row seat to the godly example of his own father, Seth. But God has no grandchildren! While Seth could pass on a godly heritage, Enosh could not inherit a personal relationship with God. That had to be his own choice. And living in the midst of an increasingly godless civilization, Enosh made that choice. When he did, others seem to have followed his lead. I wonder whether his friends and neighbors worshipped individually. Or did they join Enosh in corporate worship? All we are told in Scripture is that it was during the lifetime of Enosh that "men began to call on the name of the LORD."[2]

The Community of Worship

The implication is that a small group of men, surrounded by a rebellious civilization, separated from the crowd as they followed Enosh's example. They must have drawn strength and encouragement from one another.

I'm grateful that I had a godly heritage that involved corporate worship expressed in regular churchgoing. In fact, I can't remember a Sunday when I was living in my parents' home that we didn't go to church. When I married Danny Lotz, he laid down one of the foundational rules for our marriage: every Sunday we would be in church unless we had a fever or were throwing up. That rule also applied to our children. And we didn't go to church just for the worship service on Sunday. We were involved in Sunday school, Bible studies, fellowship socials, committee meetings, and prayer vigils as we fully embraced corporate worship.

In the fellowship of the local church, I learned reverence for God. My grandfather was the "enforcer" and would tolerate no squirming or cutting up—especially during communion. All it took was a sharp look from him, and I froze. In the fellowship of the local church, I learned to praise God through music, singing hymns that seemed in themselves to be inspired, even though I remember as a girl thinking at times that the soloist sounded like a cat whose tail had been stepped on. But to this day, I love the old hymns. In the fellowship of the local church, I learned the doctrine of God's Word, underscored by reciting the Apostles' Creed or the Nicene Creed every Sunday. And through my involvement in the local church, I learned to serve the Lord, leading my friends to faith in Jesus. In the fellowship of the local church, I spoke at the age of seventeen for the first time from the pulpit when my pastor asked me to share my testimony.

What has been your church experience? As vital as the church has been in my spiritual and theological development, as with any gathering of fallible humans, not everything in my experience has been ideal. To be honest, at times I have been deeply wounded by the churches to which my husband and I belonged.[3] So I understand if your experience has been negative. However, we live in a country where, in most areas, there are several churches to choose from. It's well worth the effort to find a church that loves God, believes His Word, proclaims His gospel, and seeks to effectively pass the Baton to those who come within its fellowship.

Living in the midst of a wicked, rebellious, hostile civilization, we must worship God with those who also worship Him in Spirit and in truth.[4] It is not an option—we must. God has placed us in the body of His Son because we need one another if we want to maintain the fire of our faith, the strength of our commitment, the zeal of our love, the faithfulness of our service, the consistency of our obedience, the depth of our surrender.[5] While circumstances may dictate that you worship without a supportive church fellowship, it becomes more difficult to maintain the sharp edge of your commitment to serve the Lord and the fervency of your love for Him.

I was reminded of this recently when I stayed in a little mountain cabin that had a fireplace that burned real logs. I noticed that if a log became separated from the other logs, the fire in that log went out. In order to burn, it had to stay close to the other burning logs. The same is true of our faith. If our hearts and lives are to remain on fire for God, we need one another.

The Consuming Zeal of Worship

Genuine corporate worship is contagious. This is underscored by a thrilling scene described for us in Revelation 4 and 5. The Lord God is seated on the throne at the center of the universe. "In the center, around the throne, were four living creatures. . . . Day and night they never stop saying: 'Holy, holy, holy is the Lord God Almighty, who was, and is, and is to come.' Whenever the living creatures give glory, honor and thanks to him who sits on the throne . . . the twenty-four elders fall down before him who sits on the throne, and worship him."[6]

Then the apostle John testified, "I looked and heard the voice of many angels, numbering thousands upon thousands, and ten thousand times ten thousand. They encircled the throne and the living creatures and the elders. In a loud voice they sang: 'Worthy is the Lamb, who was slain. . . .' Then I heard every creature in heaven and on earth and under the earth and on the sea, and all that is in them, singing: 'To him who sits on the throne and to the Lamb be praise and honor and glory and power, for ever and ever!'"[7]

The worship, which begins with the four living creatures at the throne, ripples out to the twenty-four elders, then cascades to millions of angels until the entire universe rocks in praise! Everything and everyone that has breath roars in acclamation of the One who alone is worthy "to receive power and wealth and wisdom and strength and honor and glory and praise!"[8]

Public worship must arise out of a private, intimate, authentic relationship with God, or it can become perfunctory and religious. Just a tradition with rituals to keep. For worship to be contagious, it must also be personal. From the heart. Based on a vibrant faith, rooted in the truth.

How would you describe your worship? Is it mechanical or heartfelt? And what does heartfelt worship communicate? What role does it play in effectively passing on the Baton of Truth? Let's find out . . .

8

A Love for the Word

It was a snowy night at my grandparents' house in the mountains of North Carolina. I could hear the wind whistling around the eaves. When I glanced outside, the courtyard looked like a snowy ballroom as the floodlights glittered off the icicles hanging from the gutters.

Morrow and I, both in high school at the time, had come up for a weekend visit with Daddy Bill and Tai Tai, not knowing we would get snowed in. Now we were headed back to their room for devotions with the two of them.

The fire was roaring because Tai Tai had just stoked it. The crackling and popping of the burning wood added to the coziness of the room as snow fell heavily outside the windows. The four of us climbed up on the big bed, and Daddy Bill opened his Bible and read from it. We had a sweet time discussing the passage and praying together.

This particular evening stands out in my mind, partly because Tai Tai was utterly delighted to have us holed up in their house but also because this was the only time I remember it being just the four of us cozied up together on their bed. Daddy Bill was so often gone during my younger years. However, of all our countless visits through the years, I never remember one when we didn't discuss the Bible in some way. I definitely inherited my grandmother's love for snowy days and coziness, but more than that, I inherited her—and Daddy Bill's—love for the Word of God.

Tai Tai always had more than a dozen Bibles in different translations scattered around her bed and desk. She would compare passages in order to enrich her own study and understanding. She cherished God's Word! She filled every free space within her Bible with quotes or thoughts or references to other passages. A true student of the Word, she was surely one of God's most spongelike pupils. What an impression her love for the Word made on me, and that impression remains fresh in my mind even though she has been gone for too long.

In fact, all four of my grandparents as well as my parents passed on to me a deep love and respectful awe for the Bible. They showed me that it is not an old book that is hard to understand. It is the Word of God, alive on every page and in every word. As Tai Tai wrote on the flyleaf of the Bible she gave my mother on the day of her baptism at the age of nine, "The Bible is your one sure guide in an unsure world."

Daddy Bill preached the gospel all over the world from the pages of his Bible. When he was at home, I saw him studying his Bible, writing notes, looking into the Scriptures for his next sermon. He didn't just get up and preach his own words; his sermons came from his love and study of God's Word. In their home, a Bible could be found in every room so that anyone would have easy access to it. God's Word was central to their home and lives. Every meal that I ever ate with Daddy Bill ended with devotions. Just as he did that snowy night, he would open his Bible and read a passage, and we would discuss it. Many times he would turn to a psalm.

As my grandparents grew older and their vision weakened, they kept notebooks filled with passages of the Bible printed in large type so that they could continue studying Scripture. One of the sweetest privileges of my life was reading Scripture aloud to Daddy Bill as he grew older. I was always eager to share and discuss a passage I had been studying, just to hear his thoughts on it or to possibly even encourage him.

My Grampa Lotz loved the Word as well. As I mentioned previously, he was a pastor in the Bronx. He spent almost every waking hour, when he wasn't sharing the gospel with someone, studying Scripture or reading books about the Bible. His Bibles were so well read and studied that they were falling apart. He kept a wide elastic band around them to keep the pages from falling out.

As he grew older, his vision weakened also. I'll never forget the image of Grampa Lotz leaning over his Bible with his face close to the page, holding a magnifying glass so that he could see the words. He died when I was twelve, but even as a young girl, I knew he was a man who loved and cherished the Word.

One evening he asked me to sit next to him on the couch. He was a very large man, a former wrestler, with a thick New York accent. He told me to open his Bible—which he pronounced "the Woid of God"—and read to him the seventeenth verse of every chapter, starting with the book of John. I continued turning to verse 17 in every chapter and reading aloud until I heard him start to snore. Gramma, who was sitting in the room sewing, motioned for me to quietly leave. The second I moved from the couch, Grampa told me in a booming voice, "Sit down! Keep reading." I don't remember what all the verses said or why he chose them, but I do remember it was important to Grampa to hear me read the Word out loud.

Gramma was a hardworking Italian American believer who could have stepped out of the book of Acts. When she wasn't working as a hygienist in her Fifth Avenue dental office, she was helping people in their church. She fixed meals, sang in the choir, and greeted people in such a warm way that everyone felt at home. I remember my mom remarking that when Gramma came into the house, she brought the sunshine.

My mom tells of a temper-testing moment when she, Dad, my older brother and sister, and Gramma and Grampa were driving to Cape Cod from New York City and had just experienced their fifth tire blowout. While everyone else in the cramped car was hot and frustrated, Gramma started reading the book of Revelation out loud to no one in particular. My mom heard God speaking to her through the passage Gramma was reading: "I know your deeds. See, I have placed before you an open door that no one can shut. I know that you have little strength, yet you have kept my word and have not denied my name."[1] In that very moment, as Gramma read, my mom knew God was calling her to teach Bible Study Fellowship. BSF had previously turned down my mom's request to start a class, but she knew God was telling her He would open that shut door. And He did! God used Gramma's love for the Word to provide the confirmation my mom needed to step out in faith and reapply. As a result, thousands of people who studied the Word under my mom's leadership were blessed as they either became genuine Jesus Followers or were encouraged and challenged to go deeper in the Word as longtime Jesus Followers.

My dad's love for the Word blessed our family as well. We used to joke that no matter what we shared with my dad, whether it was about school or friends or dating, he never directly helped us with our problems. Instead, his response always started with "The apostle Paul would say . . ." By the time he finished telling us about Paul's ministry, we had forgotten what we asked him about in the first place. Problem solved!

As much as Dad loved the apostle Paul, the Old Testament was his real love, and he passed that love on to me. Neither of us could ever get enough of the stories! He loved the battle scenes and the righteousness of God's judgment on those who didn't obey His law. He loved reading about Elijah's boldness and David's toughness, Daniel's courage and Abigail's humble winsomeness. Dad famously used to ask audiences at churches or conferences how many of the original people who fled Egypt actually made it into the Promised Land. People would throw out all kinds of large numbers, and then Dad would tell them it was only two: Joshua and Caleb. Or he would urge someone in his Sunday school class to go home and memorize Hezekiah 3:8. The person would make a serious commitment to do so, only to find, of course, that there is no Hezekiah 3:8! It was Dad's way of getting across to his class that they needed to memorize the books of the Bible.

On many occasions, I came down late at night after doing my homework and found him in his study, which was the size of a closet. The walls of the tiny room were covered with bookshelves, all filled with Bibles, commentaries, and books about the Bible that he never tired of reading. As Dad grew older and his health deteriorated, decreasing his mobility, he often sat and read his Bible for hours at a time. He spent much of his free time preparing for two Bible studies that he taught up until the day he went to Heaven. Dad wasn't eloquent or seminary trained. When he got up to speak, it was like watching and hearing a warrior out of the Old Testament. His presence spoke almost as loud as his words. I miss him, but I am so thankful for how he invested in my life by always turning everything back to God's Word.

Both sets of my grandparents and my dad played a vital role in cultivating my love for God's Word. But hands down, the one who has most influenced me to love, cherish, and rely on my Bible is my mother. Growing up, when I would come down the stairs in the mornings, I would find her either on her knees praying or studying her Bible. From that study has come a wealth of wisdom and knowledge that has gotten her through many major storms and has also equipped her to counsel me through my storms. The Bible is as much a part of her as breathing is. She loves the Bible with all her heart, and that love is evident in how she lives out what she learns in humble obedience.

As I observe how my mom immerses herself in the Bible, I feel like I get to witness what someone is like in Heaven, living in the presence of God. It's as if she is already there. Problems don't matter, sickness doesn't matter, an unstable world doesn't matter, because her eyes are on Jesus, her loving heavenly Father . . . through the pages of His written Word. I want to join her!

The example God has graciously given me through my grandparents and parents is one that I want to emulate. So I rise early in the mornings to pray and study my Bible. I spend hours studying the Word in preparation for teaching a weekly Bible study. My girls have grown up seeing me in my Bible on a daily basis. They gather around and do their homework while I work on Bible study. Often

I'll stop and share something the Lord has shown me. Not a day goes by when we are not talking about a passage of Scripture that encouraged us or a story that intrigued us. I want my girls to be saturated in God's Word, which means I have to be too. One of Tai Tai's quips was "You can't teach your children to love spinach if every time they see you eating yours, you gag." While funny, that's true! Our children learn more by what they see us doing than by what we tell them.

If I told people that I loved someone but they could see that I often refused to listen to him, dismissed his advice, and didn't care to spend time with him, those people would emphatically disagree with my declaration of love for him. It's one thing to say I love someone, but it's another thing to actually live out my love for that person. If we truly love God, then we will love His Word. We will be eager to listen to what He has to say.

So when is the last time you opened your Bible? If your reading has become stale, would you ask God to refresh it? He can make it come alive to you.

CREATING A LEGACY OF WORSHIP

What view of the Bible are you passing down to your children? As your children, your friends, or your coworkers look at your life, what do they see as being important to you?

Be a Jesus Follower: *Read, study, apply, obey, and love God's Word.*

These are the commands, decrees and laws the LORD your God directed me to teach you to observe . . . so that you, your children and their children after them may fear the LORD your God as long as you live by keeping all his decrees and commands that I give you, and so that you may enjoy long life.

Deuteronomy 6:1–2

9

The View from the Top

My parents and grandparents have taught me through their example to spend personal time with the Lord every day. But it's not easy. The enemy knows how to distract me from my prayer time with texts, emails, social media, news, phone calls, crying children, busy schedules, chaos, and late nights that lead to morning exhaustion. And sometimes he uses my fear that I won't hear from the Lord to keep me from even trying to listen.

The difficulty I've experienced in establishing and maintaining a morning devotional time seems to be illustrated by a story in Matthew 17. Jesus took three of His disciples and "led them up a high mountain by themselves."[1] It wasn't just a mountain but a high mountain. It would have taken a lot of effort for them to get alone with Jesus, and I think that was one of the points Jesus was making. But because Peter, James, and John made the effort to climb the high mountain and get alone with Jesus, they experienced a fresh vision of His glory in a way they never would have otherwise.

That story reminds me of the hikes I used to take around my grandparents' home as a kid. Their house is nestled in a mountain cove of western North Carolina. It was built on land that was carved out of the mountainside. As I gazed at the mountains all around the cabin, they would take on different shapes, with ridges and ravines casting shadows that changed with the seasons and the time of day and the clouds that rolled by. The trees stood tall and thick, having survived years of swirling winds and bears sharpening their claws on the trunks. Birds of all kinds nested in the thick vegetation. Their singing in the mornings was so loud that, without fail, they woke me up earlier than I had planned. Tai Tai loved flowers, and she cultivated them in such a way that they looked wild, not planted. The fresh air was delicious in the fall and winter and spring but as thick and humid as a rain forest in the summer.

My mom especially loves the mountains, loves to hike, and loves all things outdoors. To look at her, you might not think she loves to dig in the dirt and plant flowers or take a walk every chance she gets, noticing every bird and recalling the species of each tree, bush, and flower along the way. Often, when we would arrive at my grandparents' house, she would want to go on a short hike within minutes of unpacking. She tells me she spent much of her childhood exploring every inch of the mountains around my grandparents' house from the Bear's Den (a rocky cave), to the laurel thicket, to the apple orchard, to the ridge, to Big Whiskers (named for the icicles that cover the rock face in the winter), to the Reed Field. She even buried a memory capsule somewhere on the mountain when she was a girl. I searched every crevice as a kid, hoping to find it, but with no luck. Now she doesn't know where it is either. I may not have found Mom's memory capsule, but like her, I developed a sense of wonder and worship—love for God's creation and awe at His handiwork. I did not, however, get her green thumb!

I always loved to hike to the ridge above my grandparents' house. When we were growing up, my mom would make my brother, my sister, and me put on blue jeans to protect our legs from briars, rocks, and ticks. She then retrieved the key that opened the gate in the tall fence surrounding some of the property. After turning the key in the lock, we all had to push away piles of leaves and any dirt that had built up from small mudslides so that the gate could actually swing open. Once through, we began the steep hike.

I remember on several occasions having to carefully step around snakes that had been sunning themselves on rocks or were curled up under a bush. We were taught to watch our step and to never barrel through the woods or grass or climb over rocks willy-nilly. It wasn't just snakes that could cause problems on the hike but old, rusty barbed wire that was half-buried and camouflaged by leaves and weeds. Halfway up, we would pass the old Bear's Den, always hoping it hadn't been reinhabited!

With the ridge in our sights, we dug our feet into the side of the mountain, step after step, quads burning and sweat pouring, until we reached the ridgeline. As hard as it sometimes was, the spectacular view was always worth the effort. I could see for miles! The view from far below was nice, but it just never compared with what I could see from the top. The breeze was always strong and cool along the ridge. I could follow the shadows of the clouds across the whole mountain range. The view gave me a new perspective on the name Blue Ridge Mountains, because I could see the blue tint. What I would have missed if my mom hadn't opened my eyes to the view from the ridgeline!

Which brings me back to the lesson I've learned about daily personal devotions. There is so much God wants to show me and teach me through His Word, if I will just commit to spending time with Him each day. He can guide me in whatever I am facing as a parent, a spouse, a teacher, a neighbor, an athlete, a ministry leader, or a counselor. It was through my personal devotional time that God prompted me to continue dating the man who is now my husband. It was through my personal devotions that God confirmed to me it was time to have children. It was through my personal devotions that God led me to start teaching a Bible study.

Time and time again, He has used His Word to encourage me, give me a warning or a promise, or convict me of a sin. I recognize God speaking to me through a particular passage when my heart starts racing and my breath seems to catch, like an aha moment.

Usually it's when I open up my Bible and God addresses the burden on my heart or answers the question I just posed in prayer. Sometimes He speaks to me about something I hadn't even voiced. And He always speaks in the most perfect way, not haughty or rude or eager to punish. He is our Good Shepherd. As the praise song says, *He is a good, good Father.*[2]

I've watched my mom devote every morning of her life to studying God's Word and praying, just as she saw her parents do, just as her parents saw their parents do. My mom remembers as a little girl seeing her grandfather (Tai Tai's father) on his knees in prayer beside his rocking chair, where he had been since 4:00 a.m. When he died, my great-grandmother found his prayer list, which was pages of single-spaced typed names that included the names of my mother's friends.

My mom makes a point of going to bed early so that she has the strength and energy to get up early and spend time with Jesus. Tai Tai used to stay up late and still get up early to spend time with Jesus. Some people need more sleep than others, but no matter what, we all can choose to get up and invest time in God's Word.

After all these years of my mom thoroughly studying God's Word, sometimes focusing on just a few verses a day as she works through a book in the Bible, I can see the clear evidence of that study. She is the wisest, godliest woman I know. Tai Tai was filled with wisdom as well, which came from her study of God's Word.

My mom has told me that I must set my spiritual compass each morning by praying and studying my Bible so that my heart is lined up with God's will and His Word. That way, during the day, God can bring back to my mind what He has said. Because of that time spent with Him, I'm less likely to be impatient with my kids, I'll make wiser decisions and be better at counseling my kids, I'll have more humility when in a disagreement, and I'll have peace when things start to go crazy. I know this because the opposite happens when I don't spend time with the Lord. I feel emotionally, mentally, and physically beaten up at the end of the day, only to realize that I didn't set my spiritual compass that morning.

Of course, we can't inspire those around us to spend time in God's Word if we don't do so ourselves. Let's remember that our kids are watching.

I am resolved to set my spiritual compass in the mornings, which requires not just a one-time decision but following through one step at a time until I can enjoy the view from the top.

CREATING
A LEGACY OF WORSHIP

What priorities need to change for you to spend daily time in the Word, setting your spiritual compass and gaining perspective for each new day?

Be a Jesus Follower: *Start your day with God.*

Jesus took with him Peter, James and John the brother of James, and led them up a high mountain by themselves. There he was transfigured before them. His face shone like the sun, and his clothes became as white as the light.

Matthew 17:1–2

10

Seek Ye First

P arents experience so much pressure to help our kids succeed in every way, especially in sports and other extracurricular activities. Often homework is rushed through while family meals, sleep, and even church are sacrificed on the altar of achievement. God is pushed to the margins, even in Christian homes. In raising our girls, we've wrestled at times to balance our family values and the demands of the basketball court or soccer field. The unwavering standard set by my Grampa Lotz convicts me to check my own priorities against those of God.

My grampa lived among people who were in need on a daily basis. His heart was for the people of New York City. After starting several churches on Long Island and in Brooklyn, he pastored a church in the Bronx, as I mentioned earlier. He also preached on street corners throughout the city, led a Bible study for homeless people and others in the local McDonald's, witnessed to commuters on the subway, and passed out gospel tracts by clipping them to dollar bills because he knew that way they would be accepted.

During my dad's childhood and teen years, Grampa was involved at the Bowery Mission, which serves the homeless of New York City by providing meals, clothing, and shelter. He preached regularly in their chapel to an audience of mostly men who were dealing with alcoholism. On Friday nights my dad joined him at the mission, playing the trumpet before Grampa preached. The men in the audience weren't the only ones whose spiritual perspective was challenged by Grampa's commitment to those Friday night chapel services.

One week my dad was thrilled to learn he was the only freshman to make the varsity basketball team at Northport High School. His house was right across the street from the school, so he didn't have far to go to tell his parents the great news: he would be in the starting lineup on Friday night!

Grampa responded, "Dan, don't you remember what Friday night is? It's the night you promised to play your trumpet at the Bowery Mission. I'm sorry, but you're not going to play in the game or even go to it."

My dad must have felt as if he'd been punched in the stomach. I can imagine that the blood drained from his face, his heart started erratically beating, and he had to bite his tongue hard to resist the temptation to talk back. My grampa would not tolerate any disrespect from my dad or his three brothers. But no doubt, my dad was fuming. The fact that my dad told me this story hundreds of times is evidence that it really affected him.

Even though my dad's initial reaction was anger, he obediently walked into the Bowery Mission chapel on Friday evening, stood at the front, and played his trumpet, knowing that at that moment the game was getting started. Grampa gave his message, then invited men to come to the front for prayer. Dad witnessed broken men streaming down the aisle to ask for prayer, including a once-wealthy businessman who now lived on the streets because of alcoholism.

In the car on the way home, Grampa reminded Dad that God's Word says to "seek ye first the kingdom of God, and his righteousness; and all these things shall be added unto you."[1] Grampa told my dad that if he would always remember to seek the Lord first in all that he did, God would take care of everything else. Grampa also observed that God hadn't made my dad six feet, seven inches tall and given him amazing athletic agility just so he could play tiddlywinks!

My dad went on to start on his basketball team all four years in high school. He received a full scholarship to play basketball at the University of North Carolina, where his team won the 1957 national championship. The following year, he captained the team. When he graduated from UNC, he still had one year of athletic eligibility left. So he tried out for the football team, made it, and was given a full scholarship during his first year in dental school. After dental school he joined the air force, where he made the all-service basketball team and was invited to try out for the Olympics.

Considering how God led my dad to North Carolina where he would meet my mom, fall in love at first sight, then marry her, and looking back on Grampa's memorable words to my dad, I wonder, could it be that so many of those blessings in love and sports came from sacrificing his first night as a starter on the basketball team? What would have happened if my dad had played basketball that night instead of serving the people at the Bowery Mission? I'm so thankful that we will never know. God has certainly honored his sacrifice!

Grampa was a Jesus Follower, and he strived to raise his boys to be Jesus Followers, which meant putting the Lord first. As a father, Grampa had enough wisdom and courage to teach my dad an important but hard lesson that night. I don't think Grampa ever even considered allowing Dad to skip playing the trumpet at the Bowery Mission.

As a parent, I find myself challenged by his firm conviction. My middle daughter, Sophia, has been a successful athlete, having played three sports through middle school and most of high school. Eventually she worked her way up the ranks on highly acclaimed club soccer teams while continuing to play soccer, tennis, and basketball at school. Her height, athleticism, and thin, agile frame set her apart from other goalies. She received dozens of recruiting emails and letters from colleges all over the country. She devoted all her time outside school to playing goalkeeper to the best of her ability. During varsity basketball season, some days she would have 6:00 a.m. basketball practice, go to school, and then race over to the soccer fields across town for her 4:00 p.m. club goalkeeper practice, followed by a 6:30 p.m. team practice. She would then come home at 8:00 p.m., do her homework, and start it all again the next day. We sacrificed money and time and even church on some Sundays in order to give her every opportunity to excel. She maintained a 4.4 GPA, showing that she thrives on discipline. But God had different plans for her life's direction.

Sophia has always had an unbelievable ability to catch anything that's thrown at her. But she has thin, small-boned, fragile fingers. While her hands are beautiful, her fingers have broken so many times that I am not sure we have even kept count. Our eyes finally began to open to the cost of chasing a high-stakes Division 1 offer, which had kept us in somewhat of an overdrive stupor. The turning point came when, after losing in the state championship the weekend before, Sophia participated in a goalkeeper showcase where a lot of college coaches came to watch and potentially recruit. I was fortunate enough to see one of her last incredible saves. On this occasion, a former male pro player kicked the ball full force. Sophia, with lightning reflexes, leaped and made a textbook save, tipping it over the top of the goal. The head of goalkeeping for the club saw the save and uncharacteristically jumped up and down, yelling his approval.

Sophia executed a couple more saves before the showcase ended and she headed my way. Like a lot of athletes who have endured years of bumps and bruises and blows, she hides her emotions well, so I didn't know anything was wrong until she held up her hand and her middle finger flopped. It just hung down, and she wasn't able to lift it, bend it, or move it at all. After an evaluation by the trainer, followed by a visit to a hand specialist, it was determined that she had completely severed all her tendons in that finger. Best-case scenario, it would be a nine-week recovery, keeping it in a splint at all times. If she were to remove it from the splint even briefly, the whole process would start over and might require surgery. To make matters worse, she had just made the starting lineup on the varsity basketball team.

When the nine weeks were almost complete, the doctor talked

with us about the risk of continuing to play soccer. From all the injuries, Sophia's hands hurt on a daily basis even when healed. He allowed it to be Sophia's decision, but he strongly suggested that she not continue to play because of long-term effects. As we faced this difficult reality, I couldn't help but think of the life lesson Grampa had ingrained in my dad.

As I reflected on all those years of training, tournaments, weekend games, missed church services, lack of sleep, zero social life, difficult teammates, thousands of jarring dives onto the ground, concussions, pulled hamstrings, and broken fingers, as well as dragging my other two daughters here and there and everywhere—all of which now seemed to be coming to an abrupt end—I had to ask myself, *Were we seeking first the kingdom of God?*

I realized that what my grampa did for my dad by making him give up his first starting game as a varsity basketball player in order to keep his commitment to the Bowery Mission was nothing short of amazing. His insight challenges me to remember that, even in today's world, we are called to seek the Lord in all we do if we want to ensure we are in His will.

Do you find yourself similarly challenged by what your family priorities indicate about the center of your worship? If you find yourself losing your temper at your child's games, feeling frustrated by her game performance, losing sleep over her lack of playing time, shoving her into one more practice when she is about to collapse, or making her play another season even though she isn't as passionate about the sport as you are, then it's time to check your heart. I've struggled with all those things at one time or another. I've had to ask myself, *Does my heart align with God's heart and His desire for my child? Do I truly want God's will for my child, or are my goals for her more important? Is my child growing in her relationship with the Lord as much as she is growing as an athlete?*

As you and I strive to pass on our faith, we need to consider what our priorities reveal about what or who is the focus of our worship. Whether stewarding our own God-given skills or guiding our children in developing their talents, we are called to seek the Lord first. Before any tryouts, before any decisions about injuries, before any career or college choices, we should be asking God what His will is, seeking wisdom from His Word. As we listen carefully for His leading, we also have to commit ourselves to obeying without question, whether or not it's what we want. Our choices signal to a watching world where our hope truly lies.

We struggled to decide whether Sophia should quit soccer when she was so good at it. But as she prayed, God gave her this verse: "See, I am doing a new thing! Now it springs up; do you not perceive it?"[2] She knew God was saying He had something new for her life. She could walk away from soccer with an attitude of worship as she trusted God to know best. I have no doubt that the discipline and calm under pressure that she learned as a goalie have been used by God to prepare her for her future.

May God bless each of us as parents, grandparents, and influencers as we choose to reinforce to our children and others around us the life lesson of seeking God first, then trusting Him to take care of the rest.

CREATING
A LEGACY OF WORSHIP

What activities and commitments is God asking you to set aside in order to make room for those that glorify Him and represent His best direction for your life and family?

Be a Jesus Follower: *Put God first.*

Seek first the kingdom of God and His righteousness, and all these things shall be added to you.

Matthew 6:33, NKJV

11

Fiddlesticks

We were already sticky because of the morning heat and humidity, making perfect landing pads for the mosquitoes to come and feast on our preteen selves. My friend and I swatted at the little bloodsuckers while we raced to the pavilion to see where we were supposed to be for our morning camp activity. The large open-air pavilion had a vaulted roof with wooden beams held up by thick wooden posts around the edges. Underneath were a basketball court and dozens of picnic tables. We zigzagged through the picnic tables and approached the list of activities pinned up by the kitchen door.

As we skimmed to find our names and learn what our day would look like, I felt something brush against the back of my hair. I shook my head and continued to review the list. Then I felt it again. I turned around and found myself facing an eight-foot-long black snake coiled around one of the thick wooden posts supporting the roof! We were nose to nose! Either his tongue or his head had been swishing through my hair! My friend and I screamed and ran as fast as we could all the way up to the camp offices. After we breathlessly explained what had happened, the camp leaders ran toward the pavilion and sent us on to our archery activity. I am sure I must have sent several of those arrows into the ground or the trees, because I couldn't shake the icky feeling of having a snake in my hair!

My parents had sent me to the Cove Camp, which was on the same property as my grandfather's training center in Asheville, North Carolina. My grandmother, mom, brother, and sister had gone to Amsterdam for the International Conference for Itinerant Evangelists, hosted by the Billy Graham Evangelistic Association. I had been really sad not to go with them to the Netherlands, so camp was the perfect distraction.

At the end of the two weeks of camp, we were to be picked up by our families in a large field by the entrance to the camp. I had assumed my dad would take off work to come get me, so I was surprised to see Tai Tai's smiling face behind big black sunglasses as she walked toward me. She had come home from Amsterdam early! Thrilled to see her, I gave her a huge hug.

Many of the campers' parents greeted my grandmother, but we finally were able to leave. I grabbed my trunk, pillow, and sleeping bag and threw them in the back of her Volvo. As we drove off, she explained that Mom and my siblings hadn't yet returned from overseas. I remember being upset and whining about how I didn't get to go and instead had to suffer through having a snake in my hair, diarrhea on a camping trip, and mosquito bites covering my arms and legs. She simply laughed and said, "Fiddlesticks!" She was basically swatting away my whining the way I had all those mosquitoes. She then urged me to tell her all about the wonderful parts of camp and about the new friends that I had made. In other words, I needed to get my mind off feeling sorry for myself and focus instead on all the blessings God had allowed me to experience.

Tai Tai focused on the positive, her glass of joy always more than half-full, even in difficult times.

Every summer when we were kids, my mom took us to my grandparents' house for a couple of weeks along with my Aunt Bunny and her kids. My Aunt Gigi stayed down the mountain with her large family, but they hung out with us during the day. You can imagine the fun and mischief all the cousins would get into. We delighted in every kind of outdoor adventure, whether we were whooping and hollering at the creative July Fourth celebration and parade in the small mountain town that my grandparents called home, hiking around the ridge above their house, swimming in the stream-fed mountain pool filled with tadpoles, or rock hopping up the creek to a place we called Monkey Bottoms. But of course, with so many cousins, on occasion we would get in a disagreement or someone's feelings would get hurt.

One summer afternoon, Tai Tai called us cousins to gather in the kitchen. I remember we were all kind of miffed. Somebody may have pegged someone else in the back of the head with a crab apple, or maybe a cousin got pushed into the creek. Who knows? But the tension had built to the boiling point. Tai Tai wanted to quickly turn our sour moods around and bring peace back into her home. She directed each cousin, one at a time, to say something nice about each of the others. After every compliment, we all had to sing her version of a song she'd learned on the mission field in China:

> Oh, you will shine.
> Yes, you will shine.
> If Jesus keeps you polished,
> You will shine.
> Through the trying storms of life,
> Through the troubles and the strife,
> If Jesus keeps you polished,
> You will shine.[1]

Of course, this did not go over well at first with the rambunctious younger crowd. Eyes were rolling and objections were vocalized, along with pleas that our moms not enforce Tai Tai's directive. But the adults presented a united front. One by one we painfully began to offer compliments to one another, followed by a less-than-stellar choir of voices whining along to Tai Tai's little song. But Tai

Tai's swift action eventually turned our pouting into praise. Just as she had when picking me up from camp, she knew how to get our minds off our problems and back on Jesus. Joy had returned!

I remember many other occasions when Tai Tai set a limit to my complaints. She would certainly listen and had enormous compassion and wisdom. But she also had the discernment to tell when I was in a whiny mood or just feeling sorry for myself. In those moments, she would tilt her head down in order to muster the deepest voice she could croak out and begin singing an old spiritual:

Nobody knows the trouble I've seen.
Nobody knows but Jesus.

Hearing that deep voice come out of such a tiny woman always put a smile on my face. She used her sense of humor and her ability to commiserate with me to gently remind me to talk to Jesus about whatever the issue was and to quit feeling sorry for myself. I've been guilty of impatiently shutting my kids down when I can tell they are feeling sorry for themselves or are just in a whiny mood. Dropping the hammer certainly stops the pity party, but it may not help their hearts recover as quickly as a sense of humor, compassion, and good old-fashioned distraction. Tai Tai was a master at all three!

It's been said that discouragement is the devil's calling card. He loves to use discouragement to divide relationships, halt effective work, and deflate us to the point that we can hardly function. We have to watch out, knowing the enemy is ultimately behind whatever is discouraging us or our loved ones.

Worshipping the Lord is the best way to fight discouragement. Tai Tai showed me three practical ways to do this: focus on the blessings in my life, carry a song in my heart, and keep a sense of humor to help remove any traces of discouragement.

Now, when I start to whine in my spirit, I seem to hear Tai Tai's lilting voice: *"Fiddlesticks."*

CREATING A LEGACY OF WORSHIP

Ask God to reveal any ways in which you've allowed frustration and discouragement to obscure your appreciation of His blessings.

Be a Jesus Follower: *Learn to laugh.*

A happy heart makes the face cheerful,
but heartache crushes the spirit.

Proverbs 15:13

12

Praise in the Midst of Pain

Turning our thoughts toward praise may be hard enough in the ordinary frustrations of life, but praising the Lord when we are in pain or physically sick is an entirely different challenge. Our human nature is to react like a wounded animal by lashing out at those around us or plunging into depression in our frustration and hopelessness. Some of us react to pain by secluding ourselves because we feel too miserable to face anyone. But if we aim to inspire faith in the next generation, our lives need to show that our hope is centered on the God who walks with us even in the hardest times.

My grandmother demonstrated so beautifully the unexplainable joy you and I can have in the midst of tremendous physical pain. Tai Tai suffered extreme chronic pain in her back and hips for half her adult life because of degenerative arthritis aggravated by a fall from a zip line she had made for my cousins. I remember celebrating my sixteenth birthday in her hospital room in Raleigh as she recovered from one of her many back surgeries. She was so joyful and excited to see me and never once complained.

One of my sweetest memories of Tai Tai took place after one of her hip replacement surgeries. My sister, Morrow, and I had to leave early in the morning after spending the weekend with her. The night before, she had insisted that we wake her up before we left. So we softly knocked on her bedroom door and peeked in while whispering her name. She woke up, and instead of grimacing from the pain she was surely experiencing, her face lit up like it was Christmas morning! She grabbed each of us by the hand and kissed us on the cheek as we leaned down. She truly glorified the Lord in her pain by thinking of others instead of focusing on her misery.

Tai Tai's example came to mind during a scary and physically painful situation God used to open my eyes to how even the worst of circumstances can provide an opportunity to worship Him.

We were driving from our home in North Carolina to visit my husband's family in Orlando. I was taking an antibiotic for a sinus infection that had also affected my lungs. I have asthma, and it had really been aggravated by this respiratory infection. My inhalers weren't helping, and as we drove down, I started to get pretty worried.

I was having my devotions in the car, and as He often does, God prepared me for what was to come by speaking to me through His Word. As I mentioned earlier, I'll often be reading a passage, and it seems to jump off the page. My heart starts pounding because the scripture speaks right to my situation or answers the prayer I just prayed. That day's reading "happened" to include Psalm 23. The fourth verse leaped off the page: "Even though I walk through the valley of the shadow of death, I will fear no evil, for you are with me." I felt like God was telling me that even though my asthma was bad, I wouldn't die from it.

Sometimes when the Lord speaks, He has more in mind than you or I realize. The night we arrived at my in-laws' house in Orlando, I found out why He had given me that verse. After going to bed, I woke up around three in the morning with sharp pain. I won't go into the details of how bad it was, but I had intestinal problems that left me on the bathroom floor, feeling like I would die any second. My husband and mother-in-law drove me to the hospital, where I went through multiple tests to figure out what was happening to my body.

While I was lying on the cold gurney, being pushed up and down hallways, then placed on tables for X-rays and CAT scans, I found that the only thing I could think or cry was "Jesus, help me!" I had no strength or desire to say anything else. Jesus was at the forefront of my mind in the scariest experience of my adult life. I was only half-conscious; my head seemed to flop around like a rag doll's. I knew my condition was serious, but I'll never forget how God brought back to my mind the scripture I had read the previous afternoon. It was as if He were speaking it in my ear. *"Even though I walk through the valley of the shadow of death, I will fear no evil."* As foggy as my brain felt, I was fully aware that God was telling me that I wouldn't die. Even though I was experiencing "the shadow of death," I didn't have to fear. Despite the scary situation, I felt complete peace. It brought comfort just to say His name out loud over and over: "Jesus . . . Jesus . . . Jesus . . . help me."

At one point, the technician had to leave the room. He was gone for quite some time. As I lay there on the cold, hard table in the darkened room lit only by the red Exit sign over the door, I whispered to the Lord that I trusted Him with my life and that I received this difficulty from Him. I actually began to praise the Lord for the pain with tears streaming down my face. It was the most worshipful experience I've ever had and one that is difficult to put into words. I felt His presence right there with me in that tiny lab room. God helped me praise Him in the middle of all that I was experiencing.

After about six hours, the worst of my difficulty cleared up, but the doctors remained baffled about what was going on. They were concerned that my white blood cell count was significantly higher than if I were having an appendicitis attack. They sent me to another room on an upper floor. A nurse came in to look at my chart, and when we started going over my meds, she paused. She noticed that the antibiotic I had been taking for my sinus infection was dangerously interacting with my asthma medicine. She said that mixing them would cause severe asthma attacks! In that moment, I realized that God had orchestrated everything. He had used my intestinal problem to get me to the hospital so that they would discover the medicine combination that could have caused a fatal asthma attack.

I spent six days in the hospital, missing my brother-in-law's wedding and the joy of seeing my girls walk down the aisle as flower girls. But God completely healed me. Not only did He use the situation to put a light on the medication, but He also taught me a vital lesson about trusting Him. When I take Him at His Word, I have the freedom to rest in His will and experience the peace that comes when I praise Him in the midst of pain.

God is present with us when we "walk through the valley of the shadow of death." He reminds us not to fear but to worship. Worship takes our eyes off our fear and turns them to the God who is sovereign over every aspect of our lives.

In one of her arena messages, I heard my mom share a powerful insight about how Jesus taught us a life lesson when He was suffering on the cross. She said that while His physical agony was beyond our comprehension, He still took care of others. He asked John to take care of His mother. He forgave the dying thief.[1] In other words, He teaches us that while our physical suffering may not be alleviated, the corresponding emotional suffering is lessened when we stop focusing on ourselves and start caring for others.

I certainly don't mean to make light of the pain or sickness you might be enduring. But in watching Tai Tai, I saw firsthand how beautiful it is to behold a Jesus Follower deliberately reaching beyond her physical pain to focus on whoever else was in the room. Because of the constant sparkle in her eyes, the smile on her lips, and the humor of her words, I believe fixing her attention on God and on others brought Tai Tai joy and helped ease her debilitating pain.

My grandmother's example of praising the Lord when in pain has inspired not only me but also my mother and my sister.

After being diagnosed with breast cancer, Mom had to undergo chemotherapy and radiation for a year, during which she suffered every side effect that might be expected and even some that the doctors had never seen before. The chemotherapy burned her hands and feet so badly that they were covered in blisters. She couldn't walk because the pressure on her feet exacerbated the problem. But like Tai Tai, my mom handled the awful pain with grace and joy.

Before every appointment and every treatment, my mom would have us ask the Lord to show us whom we needed to be a light to and whom we needed to share Jesus with. So many times people would approach my mom at the hospital because they recognized her. They would tell her what cancer they were going through, and Mom would stop right in the middle of the lobby and pray for each one.

My mom praised the Lord every day during her bout with cancer. Even on the drive to the UNC cancer hospital in Chapel Hill, she would have us praise Jesus by going through the alphabet. "He is the Alpha and Omega, Beautiful, Comforter, Deliverer, Everlasting Father, God, Holy, I AM, Judge, King of Kings, Lord of Lords, Messiah, Nazarene, Omnipresent, Prince of Peace, Quickener, Redeemer, Savior, Truth, Unmatched, Victorious, Wonderful, Exalted, Yahweh, Zealous for Us." She consistently demonstrated the beauty of praise in the midst of horrible sickness.

My sister, Morrow, has also watched how Tai Tai and Mom handled their pain with worshipful joy and selflessness. She has followed their example while suffering from daily massive migraines as well as chronic pain and chronic fatigue syndrome. She has so many food allergies that it becomes difficult to find food that doesn't cause her more pain. Her pain is so severe that it has affected both her strength and her memory. She has often missed out on normal activities because the light is too bright or the noise is too loud or the physical exertion is too much.

I've lost count of how many times I've prayed for Morrow to be healed. I'm continually amazed by how she never complains about her constant pain. Everyone who knows Morrow has witnessed her always-present, unforgettable smile. She loves to serve and is the first to jump up and grab something someone may need. She makes dinners for others who are sick and goes the extra mile to make the presentation appealing. She is my mom's travel assistant and has won the hearts of people all over the world with her efficiency and kindness. So many days when I watch her smiling and serving people, I can see her eyes dilated from a massive migraine. But no one else would know, because she has chosen to focus on others and bring glory to the Lord even in her pain.

Morrow, Mom, and I are deeply thankful for Tai Tai's invaluable example of praise through pain. Her sacrificial choice deepened our understanding of what it means to walk in worship and showed us that it is possible to exude unexplainable joy by maintaining a spirit of praise even when hurting.

Whether you are experiencing physical pain or a different sort of suffering, I hope Tai Tai's example will encourage you not to let anything take away the joy of your salvation. Just the joy of knowing Jesus. As you immerse yourself in worship and ask God to help you focus on others, I pray that He will bring you healing and renew your hope. Your choice to praise Him in your weakness will serve as a light to those watching you run your race of faith.

PHOTO BY RUSS BUSBY

CREATING
A LEGACY OF WORSHIP

Whether you are facing physical, emotional, mental, or relational pain, pray that God would give you a spirit of praise and lead you to someone who needs a reminder of His faithfulness in the midst of suffering.

Be a Jesus Follower: *Overcome discouragement with praise.*

"My grace is sufficient for you, for my power is made perfect in weakness." Therefore I will boast all the more gladly about my weaknesses, so that Christ's power may rest on me. That is why, for Christ's sake, I delight in weaknesses, in insults, in hardships, in persecutions, in difficulties. For when I am weak, then I am strong.

2 Corinthians 12:9–10

13

The God Who Is Able

As we've seen, praise isn't reserved for the days when everything goes right. Worshipping God should overflow even during our everyday busyness.

That principle was passed down by my parents and grandparents. I remember Gramma humming hymns while she was on all fours, scrubbing the floor, and I saw Grampa rejoicing when he led someone to Christ on the train, even though he was tired and low on money. I've noticed how my mom answers the phone cheerfully, even when a call interrupts her preparations for a speaking event.

Life is busy and not always pleasant, but we can maintain an attitude of worship despite the inevitable challenges.

I remember one of those days years ago when my girls were small. I was awakened by two sets of eyes staring at me. They seemed strangely eager to be awake so early in the morning. While I may or may not have been drooling in my sleep, I think I heard three questions come out of each girl's mouth, only one of which vaguely registered: "I'm hungry. Can you cook breakfast?"

I offered my standard early-morning response: "Give me a minute."

I closed my eyes once more and listened to the pattering of feet across the carpeted floor. Not two seconds later, Riggin, our six-month-old, came through loud and clear on the monitor, crying, talking, and kicking her legs so hard that she bounced on her mattress, the same noises I'd been hearing all through the night, including the seven times I had to go into her room and find her pacifier.

Finally I dragged myself out of bed and sleepily walked into my bathroom, where I proceeded to clean my eyes carefully. Pink eye had been circulating through our household for six weeks after Steven caught it in both eyes while chaperoning a ski trip for the high school he was working for. As I washed my face and brushed my teeth, I began to think how unusual it was that Riggin had been so fussy in the night. I made my way across the hall to her room and leaned over her crib, where yet another set of red eyes peered up at me above her grin, looking as if a very generous sandman had come to visit. Oh my!

This was the morning that I needed to be out the door by 7:50 in order to make it to Bell's five-year checkup at the pediatrician's office—an appointment that she should have had two months prior but that I had forgotten to schedule. As I raced through the house, trying to get everyone dressed and fed, I remembered to double-check with my sister to see whether she still was available to come and watch Sophia and Riggin while I took Bell to her appointment. At 7:41, I realized I had locked my keys in the car the night before! I grabbed the phone and called my sweet friend up the street to ask whether I could borrow her car, which had car seats. I explained that I would have to take Bell to her appointment, come back, pick up Sophia, and then take them both to preschool, hopefully on time and with their lunches. She assured me that it was fine.

I looked out the front door, and Morrow—wonderful Aunt Morrow—was standing there with a huge smile on her face, holding a Starbucks caramel steamer for me. Not surprisingly, Morrow had pink eye in both eyes! On top of that, she had a sinus infection and most certainly had one of her daily migraines. Her UNC baseball cap was pulled down over her forehead, shadowing her slightly bloodshot eyes.

As she came in, I rattled off what had happened and how I had to run down to my neighbor's house to get her car, then rush to the doctor, then rush back, then rush to school. I told her I would be back as soon as I could so that she could go home and get some rest. She, as always, said, "Take your time."

Bell and I raced down the sidewalk, jumped in my friend's car, and left at 8:08. No way were we going to be on time. Worse yet, I hadn't factored in the horrible traffic. We arrived late, and the appointment took an hour, so when I got home, I threw together some lunches and dropped Bell and Sophia off at preschool thirty minutes late. After I returned my neighbor's car, I had to borrow Morrow's car to go get my husband's keys at work so that I could pick up the girls after school. When I finally arrived back at the house, I found Morrow sitting on the floor, talking to Riggin. She had cried through her nap, and Morrow had done her best to keep her occupied, trying not to touch her because of her sinus infection. I noticed that the pile of dirty dishes I had left in the sink were now clean and put away. Such a gift!

Whew. What a morning! I know that any mother out there would agree that such chaos is the norm when you have children. Life is busy, busy, busy—and highly unpredictable!

That afternoon when I finally had a few moments to sit down, I opened up my *Daily Light,* a small devotional book given to me by my mother when I was ten. Tai Tai had given her a copy when she was ten, and my great-grandmother had given Tai Tai a copy when she was ten. I've also given a copy to each of my girls. *Daily Light* is a compilation of Scripture verses for daily reading with a theme verse at the top of each page. I cannot tell you how many times God has used that little book of verses, first published in the 1800s, to speak to me. On this particular day, the verses all focused on the theme "God is able." As I sat there contemplating my day, God began to show me how He had very ably brought me through.

Looking back on my morning, I saw how God was and always will be able to take care of this busy family. I began to praise Him for all the ways He had taken care of my needs that day. Nothing spectacular had happened, of course. I didn't make it to my daughter's appointment on time; my kids didn't show up to school on time; my keys didn't suddenly appear on the table; the pink eye didn't disappear from Riggin's eyes. But God is able. Able to provide a neighbor's car to borrow, able to get me to my child's appointment without being charged a late fee, able to get my children to school late but safely, able to free my sister up to stay a few more minutes so that I could use her car to get my husband's keys, able to gently guide me through the daily chaos. He is able!

What kind of a day are you facing? What do you see on your calendar that has you breaking out in cold sweats at night? What news did you just receive from your doctor or your child's pediatrician? What devastating financial statement just came in the mail? What are you facing? Guess who is facing it with you? Jesus. And He is able!

The ability to maintain a heart of worship in the midst of the chaos—trusting God's almighty hand to guide us through every circumstance—is necessary for passing on the Baton of Truth to the next generation. If we are constantly stressed out, worried, and faithless, then what we pass on is a bunch of anxiety. Instead, we need to worship the Lord in the midst of our busy lives, knowing that He is able.

God is able to take care of whatever you are facing, not necessarily by removing your circumstances or performing miracles but by walking with you through the day or through the crisis. If you take time to look back on all that has taken place, you will see God's able hand guiding your steps.

CREATING
A LEGACY OF WORSHIP

*Consider how you can establish a habit of pausing
each day, no matter how busy it may be, to praise God
for all the ways He's taking care of you and your family.*

Be a Jesus Follower: *Just trust Him!*

To him who is able to keep you from falling and to
present you before his glorious presence without
fault and with great joy—to the only God our Savior
be glory, majesty, power and authority, through
Jesus Christ our Lord, before all ages, now
and forevermore! Amen.

Jude 24–25

14

An Enduring Legacy

The truth of our mortality is something we all think about. Maybe we have a loved one dealing with cancer or nearing his or her last breath at the end of a long life. We think about it when we're flying on an airplane in a violent storm and when we have to slam on our brakes, narrowly escaping a bad accident. We think about it when we hear tragic stories of coronavirus deaths or rioting in our cities or shark sightings at the stretch of beach where your kids were just playing.

Though it sounds kind of morbid, death is part of the human experience. But being aware of life's brevity can prompt us to live each day with greater intention so that we leave a legacy of faith for those who follow.

While I've grieved the deaths of both sets of my beloved grandparents, my wonderful father, and many uncles and distant relatives, I've also faced the deaths of many close family friends and neighbors. I've learned that one vital key to facing death is to focus on Heaven, knowing that this world is not our home and that this life is just a momentary speck compared with our eternal life to come. Another key is to consider the gifts our loved ones have passed along for us to carry forward.

God first gave me a burden to write a book about the spiritual legacy I've been given when Tai Tai was facing death.

I'll never forget one particularly cold Saturday morning when my mother, Morrow, and I stepped into the car and headed toward the mountains to the place my mom still calls home. After three and a half hours, we drove up the long winding driveway that leads to my grandparents' house. As we reached the front door, my heart was pounding. I could barely swallow because of the lump in my throat. The tears in my eyes had to be held back. I would cry my eyes out later. For now I needed to focus on what might be the last visit I would have in this life with my beloved grandmother. As it turned out, it was.

My mom had made it clear that this was not a time for tears. It was a time to be strong. We needed to be an encouragement to Tai Tai, not the other way around. If she heard us crying or we seemed frantic, it might make her worry and affect her fragile health. We walked quietly down the familiar brick hallway, passing the large wall of windows where different-colored vases were displayed, including the vase that used to house the tadpoles we would catch with our cousins. Light reflecting off the vases cast a kaleidoscope of colors across shelves built below each row of windows.

As we turned down another hallway closer to Tai Tai's room, I couldn't help but notice her touches everywhere—the stuffed mice that peeked through the banister climbing the back staircase, bookshelves filled with beloved volumes that had been read and reread, the scent of woodsmoke that permeated the house after years of laughing fires on the hearths. Now, though, we heard the unfamiliar rhythmic beep and steady clicking of life-preserving medical equipment.

My Uncle Ned stepped through the old wooden door that led into Tai Tai's haven. He gave each of us a hug, looked into our eyes with tender compassion, and told us to take a deep breath. As we stepped over the threshold of her room, I did as he had advised. I took a deep breath and looked into the face of my beloved Tai Tai, the woman who had shaped who I am in so many ways. The woman who exemplified what it means to live for Christ, to take up our cross and follow Him. The woman who manifested nothing less than a life on fire with love for Jesus.

I walked up next to her bed, where she lay so still and so small, leaned down, kissed her beautiful face, and cried out silently to the Lord, *Oh please, oh please, oh please* . . . To form another word in my mind would have opened the floodgates of my eyes and heart. How we all loved her! How I loved her! Every ounce of this woman was precious to me. The thought of not being able to ask her how to handle a strong-willed child, how to navigate a challenge in marriage, or how to pray for a wayward loved one was unbearable. It was unthinkable that we might never again be able to share funny stories and talk about our love of clouds and art and history and books. All this and so much more still makes me weep. But most of all—most of all!—I would miss her vibrant faith in God, her contagious excitement about His Word, her deep insight into each word of Scripture, and her daily love relationship with Jesus.

Not long after that weekend, Tai Tai passed on from this life and stepped into Heaven. But God used that bedside visit to cause me to reflect on the legacy He has given me. After Tai Tai went to Heaven, I resolved to pass on to my girls the worship-filled faith I saw in her by living it out myself.

Yes, I still find it heartbreaking that Tai Tai, with so much life and wit and humor and passion and wisdom, is not waiting for me in her cabin. I won't gloss over how hard it is to lose a loved one. Yet sometimes it helps to face death as a challenge to carry on what you loved in that person.

After Tai Tai's passing, I realized I needed to make some serious choices. Would I take what she had taught me through her words and her example and ensure it lived on in my own life? Would I be that kind of example to my girls? In the face of difficulties, would I react as she had, choosing to trust God? When confrontations arose, would I use humor to ease the tension? Would I find joy in the mundane, everyday tasks of life with a smile on my face? Would I devour Scripture daily and apply what I've learned even if it's not easy? Would I treat the lowest of the low with respect and dignity? Would I wear pearls and put on lipstick every day? Ummm . . . probably not. But my answer to all the other questions was a resounding yes. Yes!

Ruth Bell Graham's beautiful influence has overflowed to my mother, to my sister, to me, and now to my girls, Ruth Bell Wright, Sophia Frances Wright, and Anne Riggin Wright. How I miss her, and how I want my girls to be like her! This desire propels me to follow Tai Tai's example and seek to offer the Lord a life of continuous, authentic worship, no matter the challenges I may face in the home, the stress of a busy schedule, the hurts that sometimes seem to multiply, or the occasional urge to quit and take a nap. It reminds me to be intentional about the choices I make every day, beginning with a total commitment to being a Jesus Follower.

That's the legacy Tai Tai left. And that's the legacy I want to leave.

PHOTO BY ADELLA THOMPSON

CREATING
A LEGACY OF WORSHIP

*Whether or not you have had the benefit of
intentional, Christ-honoring mentors in your life,
what choices can you make each day in order to
leave a legacy of worship?*

Be a Jesus Follower: *Live with eternity in view.*

Charm is deceptive, and beauty is fleeting;
but a woman who fears the LORD is to
be praised. Give her the reward she has earned,
and let her works bring her praise at the city gate.

Proverbs 31:30–31

PART THREE

Our Walk

Enoch lived sixty-five years, and begot Methuselah. After he begot
Methuselah, Enoch walked with God three hundred years, and
had sons and daughters. So all the days of Enoch were three hundred
and sixty-five years. And Enoch walked with God; and he was not,
for God took him.

Genesis 5:21–24, NKJV

While we don't know how God motivated Enosh to worship, Enosh did make that choice. And his worship inspired not only his friends and neighbors but also his family to join him. He received the Baton of Truth, expressed it during his lifetime through worship, then passed it to his son Cainan, who passed it to Mahalalel, who passed it to Jared, who passed it to his son Enoch, who went one step further in expressing his faith by walking with God. How would that be possible? While we don't know whether God appeared in a human form and walked with Enoch as a friend, we can assume that walking continually with God required effort, discipline, and strong determination.

Compelled to Walk with God

What compelled Enoch to walk with God? His decision seems to have been prompted by the awesome responsibility of parenting a baby: "After he became the father of Methuselah, Enoch walked with God."[1] When Enoch held his firstborn baby in his arms and gazed on the chubby, flushed cheeks, rosebud mouth, curling eyelashes, and little fist wrapped tightly around his finger, he must have been overcome with an intense awareness that it was his responsibility to care for his child's physical, emotional, and spiritual well-being. Did he exclaim, "How am I going to raise a godly boy in this decadent culture? I need God!" Whatever his words and emotions in that moment, that's when Enoch began to walk with God.

What about you? When did you begin to really get serious about your relationship with God? Was it a time when you, like Enoch, were overwhelmed by a sense of awesome responsibility? Was it when you held your baby for the first time, wondering how you would be able to raise him or her to be godly in this ungodly world? As your child has grown older, perhaps you feel even more overwhelmed by the responsibility of godly parenting in a world that makes sin look fun to your teenager, bombarding him or her with every conceivable temptation. Or maybe you carry the weighty responsibility of single parenting, supporting yourself and your family because of a death or divorce. You may even be a grandparent raising a grandchild. Or a teacher pouring your life into students whom you can see are headed in the wrong direction. Or a social worker confronted by every kind of suffering and abuse among children. Whatever your circumstances, has the burden planted a deep, desperate desire in your heart to draw near to God, receiving His wisdom, strength, and blessing as you help to guide the next generation?

Over time I became aware that this desperate need for God was felt by many of the women who signed up for the Bible Study Fellowship class that I taught. Prospective members always were asked to submit the reason they wanted to be in the class. Year after year, the reason given by the majority of the new class members was that they wanted to be able to answer their children's questions accurately, with biblical truth. Maybe that's one reason you are reading this book. You, too, want to raise your children in the truth, in knowledge of and reverence for the things of God. If so, walking with God is not an option. You and I must walk with Him moment by moment. Day by day.

Choosing to Walk with God

Enoch had more than just a desire to draw near to God. He actually chose to start walking with God. And he kept on walking with God every day, one day at a time, 365 days a year, for three hundred years. What a walk!

How do we apply this to ourselves as Jesus Followers? How does a person walk with God? Perhaps the best way to describe it is that it's similar to walking with a visible person.

Once a week when I'm home, weather permitting, I walk with a friend for two and a half miles. We abide by two basic rules when we walk together. The first rule is that we must walk at the same pace.

The second rule is that we must walk in the same direction. If we don't follow the rules, we can't walk together. The same two rules apply when walking with God.

If you and I want to walk with God, we have to walk at His pace, which means moment-by-moment obedience to His Word. How can we obey God's Word if we don't know what it says? And He has said so much, I find I have to read it every day to keep up with Him. Ignorance, neglect, or willful disobedience of God's Word will cause us to get out of step.

We also have to walk in the same direction God is walking, which means moment-by-moment surrender to His will. We can't go off in a direction of our own choosing. We must surrender our lives to Him, letting go of our own plans and goals and ambitions. We just give everything to God. We reach the point where we are able to say, *God, I want what You want more than what I want. I surrender my life to You. Your will is mine; Your goals are mine; Your priorities are mine.* This is the only way we can walk in companionship with God. Step by step, moment by moment, day by day, year by year, for the rest of our lives.

What adjustments do you need to make so you can walk with God? Adjustments to your daily and weekly schedules? Adjustments to your attitude and ambition? Adjustments to your personal habits of prayer and Bible reading? You and I cannot walk with God if we don't know what His pace is or in which direction He is going. And the only way we can know His pace and direction is to prayerfully read His Word. I can testify from personal experience that the time and effort required are more than worth it.

In our fast-paced world, do you find you are just too busy to make time for prayer and Bible reading on a daily basis? If so, be encouraged. Enoch seems to have been a very busy man. Jude tells us that Enoch had something of a full-time lay ministry: he was a preacher.[2] Not only that, but Methuselah was also the first of "other sons and daughters" born to him, which meant he had many responsibilities in the home.[3] In addition, he must have had a full-time job so he could provide for his family. He may have been a nomad tending his flocks and herds or a musician or a craftsman.[4] While the Bible doesn't tell us what his job was, Enoch must have known what it was to be stressed out from an overloaded schedule. Yet he still made time every day to walk with God, one step at a time.

The beautiful result was that Enoch became increasingly aware of God's presence in his life. His habit of walking daily with God surely was not something he felt he had to do but something he wanted to do. In the process, he must have enjoyed an ever more intimate, loving, personal companionship with God. He gave God his undivided attention, spent more and more time with Him, gained a greater and greater depth of understanding, allowed fewer and fewer interruptions . . . until there were no interruptions at all and his walk of faith became sight. "Enoch walked with God; and he was not, for God took him."[5] Enoch walked right into Heaven, into the presence of God, where he still is today![6]

Timing Is Critical

So many things seem to keep us from consistently walking with God. What have been your obstacles? Weariness? Busyness? Willfulness? Pride? I understand the temptation to walk with a "limp"—up-and-down inconsistency. Maybe you walked with God in the past, but life has crowded in on you to the extent you now realize you are out of step and going in a different direction than He is.

Let me share with you one more facet of the four-by-one-hundred-meter relay race: not only must the winning team run their laps the swiftest and pass the baton the smoothest, but they must also transfer the baton in what is called "the passing zone."

In the 2016 Olympics, the American men's relay team was thrilled to finish in third place. Following the race, the team members were taking a victory lap around the track, draped in the American flag, when to their devastating shock, the scoreboard announced that they had been disqualified. The reason? The first runner, Mike Rodgers, had transferred the baton to the second runner, Justin Gatlin, outside the passing zone.[7]

I've wondered whether there is a passing zone as we seek to transfer the Baton of Truth to the next generation. For parents it seems to be when our children are young and living in our homes, under our authority and teaching. It's the time when you read them bedtime Bible stories, listen to their prayers as you tuck them into bed, take them to Sunday school and church, and play Bible games that teach them the Scriptures in an engaging way. It's the time when something unexpected and unwanted erupts in your life, and your children witness your trust of the Lord when you don't understand His ways. It's the time when they witness your faith lived out during ordinary events, day in and day out. This doesn't mean that older children can't receive the Truth, just that it may be harder for us to pass the Baton to them. One purpose of this book is to urge you to walk with God. Starting now, if you aren't already. Now. While you have the best opportunity to invite your children along.

If you've missed that opportunity and now your children are grown and gone, be assured that God can redeem what has been lost. He gave a wonderful promise in Joel 2:25 that He will restore "the years the locusts have eaten." In other words, He can make up to you the spiritually wasted years of your parenting, if that's what they were. But don't waste any more time. As you set the example of witnessing, worshipping, and walking, your children may yet receive the Truth from you. And as you walk, pray that they may receive the Baton from another runner in the race, if not you. In the meantime, ask God to connect you with others outside your home to whom you can pass the Baton.

I continue to be thankful for how Rachel-Ruth seeks to pass the Baton to her three girls and also diligently endeavors to pass it to other children whose parents aren't engaged in the race of faith. As you read the stories in this section, I trust you will be prompted to seek opportunities to pass the Baton to those within your home, as well as to others in your wider circle of influence.

15

Breaking Bread and Making Memories

The distant ringing of the cowbell Mom had picked up in Switzerland signaled dinnertime. Mom always rang the big old rusty bell when she wanted us to come home, knowing we would hear it wherever we were in the neighborhood. We would race home from playing old-timey games like Daniel Boone, Davy Crockett, and cowboys and Indians with all the neighborhood boys. Then we'd barrel through the squeaky metal-and-glass door on our back porch, pushing and shoving through the laundry room and into the kitchen to wash our hands, only then noticing how famished we were.

Mom would be dishing out spaghetti with her homemade meat sauce, toasted and buttered french bread already on the table. We'd fill our glasses to the brim with whole milk, guzzle it without taking a breath, and then get a refill before even sitting down. Dad would pray as we all held hands and closed our eyes. At least that's what we were supposed to do. Dad often peeked to see whether I had my eyes closed. When he finished praying, he'd exclaim, "Rach, I saw you peeking!" And then I would give it right back to him and say,

"How did you know? You must have been peeking too!" Dad wasn't upset in the least, but he and I always got a kick out of picking on each other.

During dinner, we would listen as Dad talked about his day and about his patients at his dental practice. Which meant he was probably talking about whose tooth wouldn't budge and how long it took to finally yank it out or how many crowns he had to put in or who hadn't paid their bills yet.

The rest of us would also share about what had happened that day, but invariably we were interrupted by the ringing of the telephone. Until I was twelve years old, Grampa Lotz never failed to call us at dinnertime.[1] The green phone hung on the wall behind me, so I was the one to answer it. Grampa always began by asking me one of two things. "How do you spell *cat*?" and after I spelled it, he would say, "Good. You're learning something. Give me to your father." Or he would ask in his heavy Brooklyn accent, "What is de secret of yo success?" to which I always answered, "Jesus!" Then I would pass the phone, stretching the twisted cord around Morrow's back to reach my dad. After my dad jokingly gave Grampa grief for calling during dinner, he would chat with him for a few minutes before hanging up and returning to our conversation.

Occasionally my siblings and I would push it a little too far at the dinner table by cutting up or picking on one another. Our parents would deliver a strong warning and apply consequences if it wasn't heeded. My brother, the strong-willed child, often found himself eating his dinner at the counter instead of at the table with us.

I, too, received my fair share of reprimands because I hated vegetables, especially squash. To this day, squash is the only vegetable I don't like. I also had trouble overchewing meat to the point that I couldn't swallow it. It turned into a ball of sawdust that I couldn't even choke down with milk. I then had to rely on my kid ingenuity. I went to the bathroom and spit it in the toilet, or I called the kitty over and sneaked him food under the table. At times my efforts failed, such as when the cat didn't like brussels sprouts or when I wasn't allowed to visit the bathroom for the third time. Dinner would end, but my mom wouldn't let me leave the table until all my food was gone. Many nights the table would be cleared, the dishes washed, and the lights turned off, but I would still be sitting there. So I did what any clever, desperate kid would: I took my wads of chewed-up, unswallowable food and stuffed them under my mom's large antique cabinet in our kitchen. My mom didn't discover my trick until years later when she had to move the cabinet. She was puzzled by the petrified wads of food she found there, but she quickly realized who was responsible. But by that time, I was out of the house and making my own menu choices.

At the end of every dinner, whether or not I was still chewing, my dad would ask me to go grab his Bible so that he could lead us in devotions. I was a pretty hyper kid, diagnosed with ADHD in fifth grade, and although I was respectful, I loved to get everyone laughing and bantering, especially my dad. He would end up saying in an exaggerated New York accent, "Rach, why is it that every time I try and say something spiritual, you change the subject?" Dad loved it. He was the king of joking around, so we fed off each other. But eventually he would return our attention to the Bible study, and we would discuss a verse. Dad would ask us questions about what we each thought the passage meant. We would try to answer but usually got the giggles again because we seemed to never give him the answer he was looking for. Eventually Dad would grow frustrated and simply declare, nearly every time, that the answer was the blood of Jesus. Until Dad went to Heaven, if one of us couldn't figure out what answer Dad was looking for during our family devotions, we just answered, "It's the blood."

Nothing super special took place at our family dinner table, but those years of eating together, sharing countless conversations marked by laughter, and discussing Scripture all had a profound impact on me.

I am now married to a head high school football coach, which means that, for over half the year, he eats dinner with us only on the weekends. My girls' soccer and basketball schedules have also complicated our family mealtimes. Often we grab fast food or find something to eat late at night when we get home.

One of the blessings of the deadly coronavirus pandemic in 2020 was that my husband, my three girls, and I were all home. For the first time in years, we consistently ate together, and the blessings were enormous. Steven was able to lead us in family devotions. The girls' interactions with him were invaluable since his normal schedule so rarely allowed them time together. And I believe it helped all of us see one another's strengths and individual significance in our family dynamics.

As much as I enjoyed the change in our family rhythm, I couldn't help but wonder what we'd missed by not previously making regular family dinners more of a priority. I realize that it's not always practical in some families, like ours, but there are other ways to set aside time for one another. We try to have one night a week where I make chocolate chip cookies and we watch a movie or play Uno. We all look forward to it.

If you, too, have been missing the beauty of connecting spiritually and personally with your family in the daily-ness of life, maybe you could set aside at least one night a week for time together—whether it's dinner or a game night or cookies and a movie. Being together will strengthen your family bonds and give your kids a sense of security, not to mention providing opportunities for unscripted conversations about living out your faith.

I'm so thankful for parents who gathered us around the table and made dinnertime memories that have lasted a lifetime. I'm now making the effort to do the same for my family, and I hope you'll join me. Let's see how God uses the simple joy of shared meals and laughter to work His good purposes in our families.

CREATING
A LEGACY OF WALKING
WITH GOD

How can you rearrange your schedule to allow for regular opportunities to share life with your loved ones and create memorable moments of joy, connection, and spiritual development?

Be a Jesus Follower: *Talk about Jesus together.*

Every day they continued to meet together in the temple courts. They broke bread in their homes and ate together with glad and sincere hearts.

Acts 2:46

16

Patience Dipped in Chocolate

Our walk with Jesus shapes how we handle what comes at us throughout our days.

What little stresses are needling you? How are you handling them? They seem to come out of nowhere and when we least expect them. Whether at work with a boss, coworker, or deadline; at home with our kids, spouse, or burnt dinner; at the store when we realize we forgot our wallet; in a car with a flat tire or dead battery; on a day when we're already running late and a friend calls to pour her heart out; or on a vacation plagued with rain, keeping everyone indoors and at each other's throats—how do we respond while staying in step with God? How do we handle these small irritations that test our sanctification?

The phrase *small irritations* brings to mind the many pets we've had over the years, which were not only sources of pleasure but also sources of aggravation that God used to develop our character.

Although I loved our pets during my childhood years, as an adult I've found them less endearing. My girls have gone through numerous pets, each of which behaved as if it were living in a barn and not a house. I've had to throw out a couch, two chairs, a duvet cover, and silk curtains! My guess on the latter casualty is that our two cats must have gotten a running start, latched on to my curtains with their nails, and then decided to relieve themselves while hanging on. It's a mystery.

As we cleaned or threw out soiled fabric, several cats and dogs came and went from our house. All too often I lost my patience with these animals. I'd yell at them in frustration, and my frayed nerves even led me to be impatient with my girls. We found forever homes for each pet we had to part with, but I'm happy to say that we now have a tidy cat that snuggles at night, even though he shows his fangs more often than his friendly side during the day.

My mom, on the other hand, adores animals of all kinds. Through-out our childhood, she nursed back to health the lame birds we found on the side of the road on our bike rides. Once, while we were stay-ing up at my grandmother's house, we discovered a baby flying squir-rel that must have fallen out of his nest. You would have thought we had come across a precious baby bunny and not a rodent! We all took turns feeding it milk through a medicine dropper. I'm sure the little guy enjoyed a long, leisurely life flying through the trees on the moun-tain, thanks to my mom's tender care.

In addition to the string of animal patients, we always had loyal German shepherds and numerous cats. I clearly remember longing, praying, and begging for a Himalayan kitten for Christmas when I was in seventh grade. My mom's parents came for Christmas that year, and on Christmas morning, my mom walked into the living room, carrying not one but two fluffy kittens—one for me and one for Daddy Bill. We were both absolutely thrilled!

As the kittens frolicked and attacked every present in the room, the doorbell rang. I remember my dad mumbling something like "Who in the world would show up at someone's house on Christmas morning? Good grief!" One look at the smirk on my mom's face, and we all knew she was up to something mischievous. Dad opened the door to find a woman holding a German shepherd puppy with a big red bow around its neck! Baby animal chaos took place after that, but it was a Christmas we will never forget.

Perhaps my most memorable childhood pet story involves my cockatiel, Murdock. He was as crazy as his namesake, one of our favorite characters from the hit television show *The A-Team*. I trained that bird to sit on my shoulder, snuggle next to my face, and walk on my fingers. My dad taught him how to do the wolf whistle, which made people feel very flattered when they walked into our house!

One Sunday my mom invited all my brother's friends over for his sixteenth birthday party. She, of course, made homemade chocolate pound cake and her famous hot fudge sauce to serve with ice cream. Murdock sat very dignified on top of his cage, watching as we scurried around the kitchen, getting everything ready for some hungry teenage boys. Apparently we had a hungry birdie as well.

The boys were laughing and carrying on in the den, seconds away from descending on the kitchen. Mom grabbed the handle of the double boiler that held the hot fudge and carried it over to the table, planning to serve the boys in a somewhat-orderly line as they walked through. I'm guessing Murdock's eyes tripled in size as he saw the steaming pot of chocolate and recognized an irresistible opportunity. He spread his wings in flight, his feet stretched out for a perfect landing, right in the pot of hot fudge! As his feathers sank into the chocolate, he discovered it was more like a pot of steaming quicksand and desperately tried to flap his way out. Mom and I both muffled our screams, and I grabbed Murdock out of the hot fudge and set him in his cage.

We could hear the boys getting ready to round the corner and enter the room. A handful of feathers stuck out of the hot fudge, looking like stalks in a cornfield. With lightning speed, Mom plucked them out, gave the hot fudge a stir, and, after shooting me a wide-eyed smile, turned to greet the first boy who walked into the kitchen.

"Hot fudge?"

"Yes, please."

I don't think there was one boy who didn't get a healthy scoop of hot fudge all over his ice cream and cake that evening. In fact, the boys were so fixated on the table of treats that they never looked up to notice Murdock sitting in his cage, preening his chocolate-coated feathers, smacking his beak, and whistling the happiest little tune a sugar-loaded bird had ever sung!

I've thought of that story a million times as I've faced stressful everyday situations with my girls, whether it was when our raucous pets misbehaved, when one of my just-potty-trained girls wet her pants while watching a parade, when running late for a soccer practice, when dealing with mean girls at school, when my parents took us out to supper and my youngest daughter threw up on the table, or when we went to the state fair and that same daughter ate fried dough, then puked all over the side of the vendor's trailer.

Scenarios like these are inevitable in family life. Each one gives us a chance to walk out our faith in real time, demonstrating that our priorities are people rather than appearances and showing the love of God even in stressful times. When we fail to maintain a positive perspective, letting circumstances rather than our unshakable hope determine our attitude, it's time to consider whether we've fallen out of step with God's priorities.

I always remember Mom's reaction to that chocolate catastrophe. She didn't yell at my bird, blame me for not controlling him, huff and puff in exasperation, or dissolve into tears, thinking the party was ruined. She was so much like Tai Tai in that situation. She showed extreme patience with me, with Murdock, and with having to serve "birdie" chocolate. She handled it with a sense of humor and a good old-fashioned quick fix.

As I reflect on that memory, I remind myself that I don't need to let stress get the better of me, not when patience and humor can defuse a situation in seconds. Then I determine once again to do my best to be patient and lighthearted, sending up arrow prayers for help when those little stresses come my way. And I picture Murdock cleaning his feathers as my brother's friends held out their plates for more hot fudge!

CREATING A LEGACY OF WALKING WITH GOD

What do you want those around you to remember about your response in the face of everyday stresses? How can you choose patience and a sense of humor over anxious thoughts and frustrated reactions?

Be a Jesus Follower: *Have patience. And remember to laugh.*

We pray this in order that you may live a life worthy of the Lord and may please him in every way . . . being strengthened with all power according to his glorious might so that you may have great endurance and patience, and joyfully giving thanks to the Father.

Colossians 1:10–12

17

Do It Scared

While so much of our faith is walked out in our everyday attitudes and actions, at times God positions us to more overtly share our faith and testimony. Heeding the prompting of the Holy Spirit isn't always as easy as it sounds.

Have you ever been so scared that you remained silent when you should have spoken up? Or remained seated when you should have stood up? Have you ever been so afraid of the consequences of sharing the gospel that you softened or compromised the truth?

At times all of us feel the temptation to back down, to not go through with it, or to let someone else do it. One of my mother's friends defines *courage* as just "doing it scared"! God often places us in situations where we need to rely on the courage He provides.

Courage is one of my mom's best attributes, but she has shared with brutal honesty how her boldness is rooted in past failure.

Mom was on a flight heading back to the United States from Switzerland. She had just attended the World Economic Forum's annual meeting in Davos, to which she had been invited as a religious leader. She felt deeply discouraged, convinced she had missed an opportunity God had given her to speak up for Him in the middle of a secular, well-educated, highly intelligent, and successful group of people. She believed she had failed at the very purpose for which God had opened the door for her to go to Davos.

But God never tosses us to the curb. He gives us more opportunities to be courageous in our witness for Him and to redeem what we perceive as a failure. God presented that opportunity to my mom on that flight. While I didn't observe what happened firsthand, her recounting of it made a lasting impression on me.

After they boarded the plane in Zurich, Mom's traveling companion elbowed her with excitement and motioned for her to look at who had just boarded the plane. My mom is never one to recognize celebrities, so the woman traveling with her had to explain that Angelina Jolie and Brad Pitt had just taken seats in the first row. Mom knew they had also been at Davos because she had passed them going into the main venue as she was leaving the night before. The entire plane seemed infused with excitement as passengers pointed to the front, whispered, stood up to get a better view, and just plain gawked. My mother curled up in her seat, closed her eyes, and spiraled down into a funk because of the missed opportunity at the annual meeting.

As the plane approached London, my mother opened her eyes. To her amazement, the people on the plane were still gawking, whispering, and pointing toward the front. She wondered, *Do people always act this foolishly around celebrities? If so, who would ever share the gospel with them?* Before leaving the States, Mom had watched a documentary on Angelina Jolie that had described the actress and the darkness that seemed to be her world. She knew Angelina needed Jesus.

Into Mom's mind came a whisper: *Anne, why do you think you are on this plane? You could share the gospel with them.*

She immediately resisted what she felt was the Spirit's nudge. *Remember me?* she objected. *I'm the failure. The one who lacked courage to stand up for You in Davos. Not me.* But the Spirit persisted.

Finally my mom relented. *Okay. I'll go speak to them.* Just then, the pilot came on the intercom and said they were making their final approach so everyone was to buckle seat belts and remain seated. With great relief, Mom told the Lord she would have spoken to them but now it was not possible. Then the pilot came back on the speaker system and announced a delay. The plane would be circling for about ten minutes.

Before she lost her nerve, Mom unbuckled her seat belt and walked to the front of the plane—straight into the lavatory! She later told me she was so scared she thought she was going to be sick.

The plane began rocking so wildly that she had to grip the handles inside the small space to keep from falling. This time her prayer was focused. *Lord, if You will steady this plane, I will go speak to them now.* Immediately the turbulence ceased! She opened the lavatory door, walked straight to Angelina Jolie, who was seated on the aisle, and asked whether she could speak to her. When Angelina graciously nodded, my mom knelt down in the aisle beside her. With Brad Pitt seated by the window, his baseball cap pulled far down over his eyes, Mom introduced herself. Then God gave her the words. She basically shared that God wanted to be Angelina's heavenly Father. That He loved her and had sent His Son, Jesus, to die on the cross to take away her sins. Mom emphasized that all her sins could be forgiven if she would trust in Jesus. That she could have eternal life, a personal relationship with God now and Heaven to come.

While Brad didn't seem to be listening, Angelina smiled warmly and thanked my mom. God used a supposed failed opportunity in Davos to urge Mom to share the gospel with Angelina Jolie and Brad Pitt, which perhaps was His plan all along. Maybe the people in Davos wouldn't have received her words anyway, but who knows? Maybe the words she shared still come to Angelina's mind and one day will bear the fruit of faith. I still pray for her.

Mom's obedience to the Spirit's direction helped pull her out of her discouragement and shame. She resolved, with God's help, she would not fail in that way again. I've seen firsthand the fruit of my mom's resolution in the years since, and one time in particular stands out in my mind.

My mom, my sister, and I were leaving Cabo, Mexico, after a weeklong vacation that had been generously given to us by a friend. Our flight had been delayed right as we were about to board. To pass the time, we walked through the little airport gift shop by our gate and then returned to our seats in the waiting area. I noticed a commotion and saw police officers escorting a small group of people through the gate that led to where our plane was parked. Morrow nudged Mom and me, pointing to a man in the middle of the entourage of security people and whispered, "I've seen that guy on the news!" Whoever he was, we assumed his arrival must have been the reason for our delay. Shortly after he boarded our plane, we did too.

We located our seats and immediately realized that they were positioned directly behind the small group with the security detail. As we got a better look at the man who seemed to be at the hub of the group, we were shocked to realize that he was the president of Pakistan. President Pervez Musharraf appeared to be traveling with his wife, a couple of assistants, and a security detail. The man sitting next to my mom, an attorney from Dallas, informed her that he had just attended an international event for attorneys in Cabo at which President Musharraf had spoken. The attorney then said he had actually gone four-wheeling on the beach with the Pakistani president the day before!

A man we assumed to be a top assistant, or perhaps even the president's chief of staff, kept smiling at us as though he recognized my mom. It's possible that, for security reasons, he had been informed of who was seated near the president and his wife, but his kind expression had us wondering whether he was a secret believer in Jesus. It's thrilling to think that God places believers in important, unlikely positions throughout the world in order to be a light for Him, like the Old Testament characters Joseph and Daniel. My mom, Morrow, and I began praying for God to lead someone to share the gospel with the president and that his heart would be opened to receive it. My mom said later that once again she seemed to hear the Spirit's whisper: *Anne, why do you think you are on the same plane with President Musharraf?*

As we exited the plane in Dallas, President Musharraf and his entourage were standing off to the side of the jet bridge. My mom didn't even hesitate. She stopped right in front of the Pakistani president, greeted him, and told him that God loved him. He seemed a little shocked but received her pleasantly with a nod, and then we had to keep moving because of the flow of people exiting the plane. Mom knew she had done her best in the few seconds she had, but she also told us that she didn't believe it was enough of a witness.

We retrieved our luggage from the carousel in a cavernous international baggage-claim hall, then got in line to go through passport control. Just then, we noticed a commotion on the escalators descending into the baggage-claim area. Here, once again, was President Musharraf, encircled by his entourage, making his way to the carousel to claim his bags! With no discussion or preamble, my mom declared that she had to go back and share the gospel with him. Morrow and I both strongly resisted. I was worried that his security would be wary of her approaching him again. My vivid imagination could see her tackled, thrown to the concrete floor, handcuffed, and taken away for questioning.

Mom paid no attention to my fears. She was focused and determined. She asked us to watch her bags, then walked back toward the carousel. The president had retrieved his bags, and the entire group was now walking down the concourse. My mom walked right up to him. At this point, my heart was beating so fast I was afraid to watch. I just knew she was about to be body-slammed to the ground! At the same time, I couldn't take my eyes off her. I saw her standing inside the circle of Pakistanis, talking with the president, who then smiled. I noticed that the man who seemed to be the chief of staff smiled the whole time she talked. We will never know whether he was mocking Mom or whether Mom's words were the answer to his own secret prayers. The president seemed to thank her as he nodded; then she turned and walked back to us.

We were dying to hear what she had said to him! By now we had lost our place in the line for passport control, so as we waited in the long queue, she had time to describe the experience while it was fresh in her mind. She told us that when she walked up, she asked respectfully whether she could speak to the president. As the men in the group stared in shock, the president said yes. So my mother shared the gospel with President Musharraf of Pakistan, one of the most dangerous men in the world at that time, a leader who supported the training of terrorist groups and threatened to use nuclear weapons against a neighboring country.

When we quizzed her to be specific about their conversation, she said she'd basically given him a paraphrase of John 3:16. She looked him in the eye and told him as sincerely as she knew how that God loved him so much He had sent His own Son, Jesus, to die on the cross as a sacrifice for sin. And that if the president would confess that he was a sinner and place his faith in Jesus, God would forgive him of all his sin and give him eternal life. She emphasized that the president could be confident he was going to Heaven when he died if he placed his faith in Jesus as his Savior. The president thanked her; then she turned and walked away, knowing she had done her best to concisely tell him the good news.

Wow! I was still shaking from what could have been. Ever since that day, I have prayed that God would bring the gospel back to President Musharraf's mind and that one day he would place his faith in Jesus.

My mom has shared that she wonders whether God used her failure at Davos to prepare her for subsequent opportunities in which great courage would be required for her to share the gospel. What she knows for certain is that her determination not to fail again led her to take the courageous step of sharing the gospel with President Musharraf.

In my mom, I have witnessed the example of someone resolved not to be concerned with pleasing people but to speak God's truth regardless of the setting or the person. She has taught me to speak the truth when given the opportunity, whether I'm having a conversation with a friend, confronting a teacher, or speaking from a podium. The response of the ones to whom I am speaking is secondary to God's approval.

When you and I are faced with opportunities to be a witness, what does our hesitation communicate to those watching, perhaps our children or grandchildren, about our confidence in the sufficiency and strength of God?

By contrast, consider what a legacy of faith we build when they see us speak up with courage and share the gospel. So let's do it scared, trusting the Holy Spirit to give us the words and strength to follow through.

CREATING A LEGACY OF WALKING WITH GOD

Pray that God would give you boldness and the words to speak the truth with kindness and grace, regardless of the setting or the person.

Be a Jesus Follower: *Speak up. Tell others about Jesus.*

Have I not commanded you? Be strong and courageous. Do not be terrified; do not be discouraged, for the LORD your God will be with you wherever you go.

Joshua 1:9

18

Red-Flag Warnings

When we're walking in step with God, the Holy Spirit may give us a nudge, an intuition, a sense of foreboding, an urgency, a strong vision of a person or situation, a burden on our hearts, a nagging feeling, a check in our spirits. We have to be careful not to ignore these "red-flag warnings." Instead, we need to take whatever it is to prayer immediately and allow God to show us how to take action, if that seems called for.

One day I received an urgent text from a dear friend who has a ministry in the Middle East. She asked me to pray, because her son and his friend were at that moment surrounded by ISIS on the border of Turkey and Iraq. This was during the height of ISIS terrorism in that part of the world. My friend's son was there for the sole purpose of sharing the good news with Muslims. When I read the text, I immediately sat down and began to pray.

Often when I pray, I envision what I'm praying for, because it helps me see and pray through every possible scenario. As I prayed, I pictured her son and his friend standing there with ISIS surrounding them. I felt prompted to pray that God would bring an

English-speaking Middle Eastern man to get them out of that threatening situation and take them to safety. I prayed with urgency and desperation.

The Holy Spirit clearly led me in prayer, because I received a text from my friend a little while later telling me that her son and his friend had escaped unharmed! I quickly texted back and asked how they had been rescued. She related that an English-speaking Turk had walked into the middle of the situation and asked my friend's son whether they were lost. The man then proceeded to lead them away from ISIS and back to their hotel. No one stopped them! They had no idea who he was. God had radically answered my exact prayer.

I hope to find out in Heaven whether that man was in fact an angel who showed up and supernaturally walked those two young men out of their dangerous situation. In response to a less-than-eloquent prayer offered by a stay-at-home mom in Raleigh, North Carolina, God took action with power and probably a host of angels all the way in Turkey. There are no limits to God's power in response to our prayers. We can go anywhere in the world on our knees!

Even though I often feel insignificant and powerless, I know God uses my prayers. I have been leading my mom's personal prayer team for the past ten years. She established a prayer team when she started her ministry, because she knew she couldn't do all that God had called her to unless she was covered in prayer. We meet once a week for the singular purpose of praying through any prayer requests she may have personally or in her ministry. The other seven ladies who meet with me are amazing prayer warriors, some of whom have been on my mom's prayer team for over thirty years.

One fall morning in Raleigh, we were praying for my mom, who was teaching her yearly seminar at the Cove in Asheville. As we prayed through each of her requests, I kept getting a picture in my head of a bear! I felt an urgency to pray that no bears would harm Mom while she was staying at a cabin on the Cove property in the mountains, especially since she loves to go on walks. Honestly, I felt a little like I was being overly dramatic, but I knew it was the Lord putting bears on my heart. The Holy Spirit was giving me a serious red-flag warning, and I needed to respond to it by praying.

That afternoon, Mom called and told me about something that had happened when she headed out for her afternoon walk. As she left the cabin, she realized she had forgotten her cell phone, so she returned to the cabin to get it. When she went back outside, she noticed a movement in the woods below the cabin porch. She quietly stood, staring at the movement, then realized it was a bear. Because my mom is adventurous, she at first thought how fun it was to see a bear out in the wild. Then, to her astonishment, she saw that the bear was heading straight for her! She immediately ran into the cabin and shut the door. The bear walked up on the cabin porch, where she had just been standing. She described him as looking deranged, like he was half-starved. He had bald patches on his back, he was thin, and he was growling. He jerked his head back and forth, sniffing the air. Then he looked into the cabin through the large window. He stood up on his back feet, growling. He actually walked around the cabin two more times, but in the end, praise the Lord, he walked away. Mom said that if she had not returned to get her cell phone, she would have begun her walk on the gravel road, and the bear would have caught her too far from the cabin for her to run to safety.

What would have happened if I hadn't responded to that burden to pray against any potential threat from a bear? How faithful God was to give me those spiritual instincts—those red flags from the Holy Spirit—to know when and how to pray.

The Lord sent red flags to my daughter Sophia one night. My oldest daughter, Bell, and I had driven to the grocery store that was close to our home. We needed brown sugar in order to make the cookies we all wanted. It was about nine thirty when we walked out of the store, and we immediately heard angry shouting about ten yards to our left. Some men were yelling into a car that was parked on the street by the entrance. They were very angry, and it was easy to see and hear that the situation was rapidly escalating. Bell and I began running to our car, as did the people around us. Everyone looked a bit panicked. Screaming and yelling, the men kept walking beside the vehicle as it started to move and then came to a stop not far from where our car was parked. It appeared that a fight was about to explode, but we didn't stick around to watch. Bell and I quickly took off and headed home.

When we arrived at the house and walked through the back door, Sophia came running down the stairs. She seemed so relieved that we were back. She then told us that she had felt a deep urgency to pray that Bell and I wouldn't get shot! We told her what had happened, and we were all in shock. The thought of getting shot wouldn't normally have entered any of our minds, because we live in such a safe area of town. Sophia could have dismissed the prompting of the Holy Spirit, thinking she was just being paranoid. Instead, she prayed just as God had led her, and it perhaps saved us from a terrible tragedy. God answered her prayer and protected not only Bell and me but everyone else in that parking lot as well. He used it as a great reminder to my girls not to ignore the red-flag warnings.

God continues to remind me to heed His prompts. At times I'll skip a particular gas station and drive to another because something doesn't feel right. Or I'll be talking to someone and get an uneasy feeling, a warning in my spirit to be on guard with that person. Or I'll be listening to a conference speaker, and an alarm bell goes off in my head, warning me that what the person is saying is not true to God's Word.

Recently, toward the end of the COVID-19 lockdown, our family had planned a trip to visit my husband's family in Florida. But the week before we were to leave, I had a strong sense that we shouldn't go. I began praying with intensity. Sure enough, God spoke to me four times from the same verse of Scripture. In two sermons, in my devotional reading and on the radio, I encountered a verse from 2 Kings: "Go inside and shut the door behind you and your [children]."[1] The result was that we all agreed to cancel our trip. To this day, I don't know why, but I'm certain God gave clear direction through His Word. About six weeks later, we felt the time was right to make the trip.

When I prayed, God answered through Psalm 121:7–8: "The LORD will keep you from all harm—he will watch over your life; the LORD will watch over your coming and going both now and forevermore."

Is God warning you about something? Could the Holy Spirit be giving you red-flag warnings to protect you and those around you? To get you to change direction or alter your schedule? Or to alert you how to pray?

In these last days of human history, now more than ever, I know I need to spend time in prayer and in God's Word, developing a sensitivity to the Spirit's warnings as I choose to heed the red flags. He is my Defender. My Protector. My Good Shepherd will lead me in the right paths if I follow Him.[2] My walk of faith is much safer when I do.

CREATING A LEGACY OF WALKING WITH GOD

Ask the Lord to give you a sensitivity to the promptings of the Holy Spirit—and the faith to immediately respond.

Be a Jesus Follower: *Heed the Spirit's warnings.*

To whom can I speak and give warning?
Who will listen to me? Their ears are closed
so they cannot hear.

Jeremiah 6:10

He who has an ear, let him hear
what the Spirit says.

Revelation 2:7

19

Set Apart

Parents, hands down, are the biggest influence on a child. Our children imitate whatever they see us doing.

I've witnessed pain, abuse, humiliation, severed relationships, and generational sin in my extended family as well as in the lives of my friends who are dealing with alcoholism. This is one area where I believe Christians need to repent of their relaxed commitment to holiness. Too many, it seems, have chosen to ignore red flags about alcohol consumption, heeding the voices around them rather than seeking the guidance of the Holy Spirit.

I have never seen my parents or either set of grandparents drink alcohol.[1] Alcohol was never in our home while we were growing up. No matter whom we were with or how important the setting, my parents never drank a drop. They were firm in their resolve to honor the Lord in every way, which for them included abstaining from alcohol.

I am so thankful that I was raised in a home where it wasn't present. If I had seen my parents drink alcohol, even occasionally, I expect I would have too. The first time I was really tempted with alcohol, I was in high school. Mom had taken my sister and me out of school so we could travel with her to Spain and France, where she would speak at several conferences and churches. A dear family friend traveling with us embraced the European attitude toward drinking alcohol, which seemed to be anytime, anywhere. I was confronted on that trip with the reality that alcohol would be readily available and mostly acceptable in the world we live in. So what was I going to do about it? Would I conform and be like everyone else, or would I follow the example of my parents and grandparents, choosing to abstain?

One of the conferences where my mom spoke was in El Escorial, Spain. At every meal a large glass pitcher of water and a large glass pitcher of wine were placed on each table. The friend we were with kept asking my mom to allow Morrow and me to drink wine at dinner. I joined in urging my mom to let me try it. The enemy whispered to me that if my mom would let me drink some wine, then I'd finally fit in at school. I'd be accepted and invited to do fun stuff. I teetered on the precipice of compromise.

Looking back, it's clear to me that I didn't truly want to drink alcohol. I was holding my breath to see whether my mom would cave and let me try it. I was testing her. Praise God! She didn't budge on her principles.

Her fortitude under pressure taught me a lesson that guides my own parenting. We as parents cannot give in. We cannot lead our children into temptation. We cannot compromise when pressured by our children, friends, family, or culture.

I ended up having my first and only sip of alcohol on that trip, during communion at a Sunday morning service where my mom was preaching. She watched from the platform as the communion wine was passed down the rows and eventually made its way to me. When the time came, I drank the little sip from the tiny cup. I looked up at my mom with wide eyes as it burned down my throat, and then I gave her a mischievous grin. She gave me a smirk because she knew I was just messing with her, but she also gave me a look that said, *Don't even think about it!*

While my parents were engaged to be married, they attended church in London with Tai Tai. The service also included communion.

My dad announced afterward at lunch, "I have a confession to make. When the communion wine was passed, I didn't drink it." Tai Tai responded with a wicked twinkle in her eye, "I have a confession to make too. When the communion wine was passed, I drank it. And I enjoyed it!"

My parents taught me to decide not to compromise in advance of any situation where I might be confronted with temptation, whether to drink alcohol, have premarital sex, do drugs, or get into a car with someone I didn't trust. That way, there would be no question as to what I would do in the heat of the moment. My decision would have been made previously.

Not only did they teach me not to drink, but they also advised me to not even hold a glass so that I would not give the appearance of consuming alcohol. Once in college, a guy offered me a plastic cup filled with beer. I said no repeatedly. He then tried to force me to take it. I knocked his hand away. The beer sloshed out of the cup; then the cup slipped out of his grip and fell to the ground. While he cursed me up and down, I just smiled and then went home. I hadn't had to wrestle with what to do when the beer was offered, because I had previously decided never to drink or hold a cup in a setting where alcohol was being served. One reason is that I don't want to cause someone else to stumble by following my example—someone who perhaps is struggling with alcoholism. A friend once confided that if she even sees someone holding a bottle of beer or a glass of wine, then that is all she can think about until she can get her hands on a drink herself.

One evening we were sitting around the table with Daddy Bill and Tai Tai after a delicious homemade spaghetti dinner, enjoying easy conversation and laughter. I asked Daddy Bill whether he had ever met some of my favorite celebrities. Cary Grant was first on my list. I've always loved his elegant, debonair characters in the movies. He said he had met him in France. Next I asked about Frank Sinatra, my favorite singer. He said he had met him several times. When President Reagan was shot, Daddy Bill and Frank Sinatra were both asked to come see him. They happened to get on the same elevator at the hotel and decided to ride over to the hospital together. They visited with President Reagan, and then Daddy Bill prayed. When he finished the prayer, Frank Sinatra said "Amen!" really loudly. Then he told Daddy Bill that he couldn't live without prayer.

Next I asked Daddy Bill about another one of my favorite actors. I could immediately tell the name didn't prompt a pleasant memory. Daddy Bill explained that he had been asked to speak at a celebrity benefit. Before the program began, everyone was mingling while drinks and hors d'oeuvres were passed around. While he was in a conversation with someone, the actor I had asked about bumped into him and spilled his whiskey all over Daddy Bill. The actor laughed and joked about it, but Daddy Bill said he didn't believe it was an accident. Although I'm sure Daddy Bill was gracious in his response, he was concerned that someone would smell it and assume he had been drinking. When he got up to speak, he told the audience what had happened. I imagine he described the incident very humorously and dramatically, because Daddy Bill was such a good storyteller. Everyone laughed! Daddy Bill's integrity was sterling. He didn't want to give the appearance—or the smell—of any behavior out of keeping with his faith. He captivated his audience with humor, resolved any possible misconceptions, and, in the process, snuffed out any gossip that could have started.

I'm aware that many Christians drink alcohol in some form. I'm also aware that challenging Jesus Followers to abstain from alcohol is not likely to be well received. But God has put this subject on my heart, and I want to respond in obedience. Could this chapter be a red-flag warning to you? Perhaps you can handle a glass of wine or bottle of beer without any issues, but does God know that the child or grandchild who is watching you cannot?

Alcohol is part of almost every occasion these days, from graduations, to career promotions, to birthday and wedding celebrations. Yet alcohol is the number one drug problem in our country.[2] It is involved in the majority of rapes and murders.[3] Car accidents are the second leading cause of death for teenagers, and unfortunately, in almost 25 percent of those fatal accidents, the teenage driver had been drinking alcohol.[4] And while the age restriction for alcohol use is well intended, it is virtually ineffective if kids can still get access to it from their own refrigerators or from their parents' liquor cabinets.

As for me and my family, we want to heed God's Word, which says, "None of us lives to himself alone. . . . Make up your mind not to put any stumbling block or obstacle in your brother's way. . . . It is better not to eat meat or drink wine or to do anything else that will cause your brother to fall."[5] Jesus told His disciples—and us as His followers, "Things that cause people to sin are bound to come, but woe to that person through whom they come. It would be better for him to be thrown into the sea with a millstone tied around his neck than for him to cause one of these little ones to sin. So watch yourselves."[6]

Alcohol is one of those areas where Christians seem to increasingly choose to be like the world rather than being set apart as light in the world. Would you seriously think about it? Are you willing to decide to abstain from it before you are confronted with the opportunity to partake? If you say you can't do that, then I would like to respectfully ask, Why? Has alcohol become more important to you than the health and spiritual well-being of your brothers and sisters in Christ? More important than the future condition of your children and grandchildren?

My reasons for abstaining from alcohol are that I never want to cause my kids to stumble, I never want to cause someone else to stumble, and I never want to put something in me that will weaken my ability to think clearly, inhibit me from hearing God speak to me through His Word, or decrease my sensitivity to His Spirit.

Will you choose to join me in setting the example for our kids, our grandkids, and others by abstaining from any form of alcohol? Who knows? You may save someone from the heartache that so often accompanies drinking, the painful realities that the enemy attempts to camouflage.

As Jesus Followers, you and I and our children are called to be set apart, not conformed to the pattern of this world. Let's live in light of that calling, keeping ourselves ready for every good work.[7]

CREATING A LEGACY OF WALKING WITH GOD

How does your attitude toward alcohol consumption and other culturally acceptable behaviors line up with God's call to be sanctified, set apart for His purposes?

Be a Jesus Follower: *Don't stumble others.*

Do not be deceived. . . . Drunkards . . . will [not] inherit the kingdom of God. And that is what some of you were. But you were washed, you were sanctified, you were justified in the name of the Lord Jesus Christ and by the Spirit of our God.

1 Corinthians 6:9–11

20

Pursuing Purity

Much like the growing acceptance of alcohol consumption among Christians, conversations around sexual morality are quickly shifting from "How can I maintain standards of holiness?" to "What can I get away with?" Certainly, the once-treasured ideal of purity seems to be undermined at every turn. Sex is splashed on almost every billboard; flaunted on magazine covers in checkout lines; sung about seductively on the radio; woven into almost every commercial, TV show, and movie; and written about in alluring detail and then celebrated in book clubs, in libraries, and on school campuses. And it's available one scary touch away on the phones in our hands and in our children's hands.

If you haven't noticed, the enemy is using sex to control and destroy our world, sinking us into a deep, dark abyss of immorality. So how can we possibly raise children to be pure? In fact, how can we ourselves live with purity at this decadent point in human history?

The answer is found in Psalm 119: "How can a young man keep his way pure? By living according to your word."[1] Being saturated in God's Word protects our minds from impurity, guards our hearts from impurity, warns us against impurity, convicts us of impurity, and makes us highly sensitive to impurity. But as my dad always said, you can't just let God's Word go in one ear and out the other. We have to read it and abide by it. We have to read it and let it transform our lives. We have to read it and love every word to the extent we apply and live it out in obedience.

The Old Testament stories give us a clear picture of what it means to be pure and what happens when we stray from God's law. Notice that when David saw Bathsheba taking a bath, he didn't turn away. He wasn't immediately sick that he had seen her naked. He wasn't ashamed when he called her to his house and slept with her. He had strayed from God's Word, from God's statutes. He was in a spiral of sin. One sin led to another until he actually sent Bathsheba's husband, one of his most trusted warriors, unprotected to the front lines of war so that he would die.[2] Where were David's red flags? Why didn't he stop the second he looked on Bathsheba from his rooftop? Had his devotion to God dwindled? Had he become lazy in his study of the Scriptures? Could it be that he was out of God's will at the time, sitting at home instead of fighting on the battlefield alongside his soldiers?

The decision to live in purity, just like the decision to abstain from alcohol, needs to be made before we find ourselves in a tempting situation. Daniel is a great example of this. As a young teenager, recently captured and enslaved in Babylon, he "purposed in his heart that he would not defile himself."[3] He decided at the beginning of his captivity not to defile himself with the king's food, which had been used in pagan worship. The same principle holds true for us. We have to decide now so that we are not wavering when temptation arises, as it surely will! And we need to train our kids to do the same.

Years before he sinned with Bathsheba, King David said, "I will set before my eyes no vile thing."[4] We have to decide to never compromise in what we put before our eyes—and then consistently live out that commitment. My parents and grandparents trained me to be careful when choosing movies or TV shows. At times, even as an adult, I've been watching a movie without realizing that it contained an inappropriate scene or sexual content. When that happens, I immediately close my eyes. I never want to become desensitized to impurity. I never watch a movie that I wouldn't let my kids watch.

My parents and grandparents never watched inappropriate shows or movies, and if something suggestive came up on TV, they promptly turned it off. They never looked at pornography, and it was never in our home. I never heard either of my grandfathers or my dad talk in a derogatory way about women. At the beginning of his ministry, Daddy Bill decided to never be alone with a woman except his wife. That meant he never got in an elevator alone with another woman, never ate dinner alone with another woman, and never had a meeting alone with another woman. He was a handsome, charming man and was away from home a lot, but he had the wisdom and foresight to set precautions to make sure he never got into a compromising situation. Even when he was at a restaurant or in a hotel lobby with my mom or with me, he would always say loudly to those around us, "This is my daughter" or "This is my granddaughter." My mother has quipped that she has been introduced to more waiters, elevator operators, hotel clerks, maids, and doormen than she can count! He made sure not to give even the appearance of impropriety. He pursued purity and integrity in all circumstances.

My mom holds to the same high standard that was set by her grandparents and parents. If she is required to be in a meeting with a man, my sister, who is her travel assistant, always joins her. I've been with my mom when men have attempted to flirt with her, then wound up embarrassed when my mom shut them down immediately.

When my girls were as young as three years old, I began teaching them about purity. I kept myself pure for marriage, and I have raised my girls to do the same. I also didn't want them to get into a situation with peers or with an unsafe adult and not know right from wrong. I've heard too many horror stories from friends to pretend that abusive situations weren't possible. Like a strong mama bear, I trained my girls to guard their bodies.

One of my daughters invited a friend for a visit when she was in second grade. After playing outside for a while, they came inside to our playroom. A few minutes later, my daughter came downstairs and said that her little friend was playing weird with the dolls. I immediately recognized the danger sign. I fed them a snack, dropped the little girl off at her house, went home, and got on my knees to pray. I knew I was going to have to talk with her mother, because I recognized the telltale signs of sexual abuse. The next day I met with the mom and told her what I suspected as gently as I could. She appreciatively received the hard information, and then we prayed together. I don't know what they found out or what was done, but because I had taught my daughters about honoring God by keeping their bodies pure and about speaking up if something didn't seem right, my daughter's little friend may have been spared a lot of pain. My daughter continued to be friends with the precious little girl until we lost touch. Even though we haven't seen them in some time, I've heard that they are doing well.

Our kids, nieces and nephews, neighbors and friends need to see us living pure lives. No kid is going to obey an adult who tells him or her not to watch a certain movie if that adult is watching it. Adults set the standard. If an adult is not living a pure life, then why are we upset or surprised when a kid follows suit? We have to live out purity in front of the next generation, we have to pray for their protection and strength against temptation, we have to nurture their relationship with Jesus so that they want to stay pure out of the overflow of their love for Him, and we have to be praying for their future spouses daily. Not a day goes by when my daughters and I aren't praying for their future spouses, asking God to keep them pure and strong against temptation.

We are in a battle! We can't let our guard down for one second. We need to choose to live pure lives, setting the example for generations to come. Will you join me as we raise a standard of purity in a wicked world?

CREATING A LEGACY OF WALKING WITH GOD

Invite God to search your heart and reveal any areas where you are not holding to His standards of purity.

Be a Jesus Follower: *Strive to be holy.*

Don't let anyone look down on you because you are young, but set an example for the believers in speech, in life, in love, in faith and in purity.

1 Timothy 4:12

21

Love Stories

I am a huge sucker for a love story! Whenever I have free time, I love to read Christian historical romance novels. My favorites are set in the Regency era in London, and I also enjoy the early American and medieval time periods. If I can't find a new one that catches my attention, then I fall back on the Graham family favorite, which is any Louis L'Amour novel. Even in his rough western good-guy-versus-bad-guy stories, he usually tucked in a romance. If you know western authors, then you're familiar with the sentiment that every man needs a woman to ride the river with. Daddy Bill, Grampa, Dad, and hopefully my husband would all say they married women to ride the river with.

If you like a good love story or need direction on the type of person you should marry or how to pray for your children's future spouses, then perhaps our family's love stories will encourage you. Because the person we decide to marry will affect not only our own lives but also the legacy we leave to our children and grandchildren. How important it is to choose wisely and to seek a godly spouse.

In an earlier chapter, I described how, after growing up in China as a missionary kid, Tai Tai traveled by herself all the way to America to attend Wheaton College. She was a normal eighteen-year-old girl, excited about the prospect of meeting her future spouse in college, God willing. She wanted to be a missionary to Tibet, so she prayed that God would have someone for her who shared that dream. Years later, she told me that she had written down a list of qualities she wanted in the man who would be her husband, and she prayed specifically for those characteristics to be present in the man God had set apart for her. She even wrote poetry about her longings for a godly spouse who would meet her qualifications.

One evening Tai Tai attended a campus prayer meeting. I'm guessing it was a rather large gathering, because it spilled over into several rooms. She heard a deep voice praying in the other room. Even though she couldn't see the person praying, she could tell he was passionate about Jesus. She silently promised the Lord that if He would let her marry a man like that, she would serve Him for the rest of her days. As you might guess, the man she heard praying was my grandfather.

However, around that time, Daddy Bill asked a woman named Emily to be his wife. Emily turned him down, observing that he would never amount to anything. What a colossal underestimation of a person! But what a blessing, ultimately, to countless people, especially Daddy Bill, given the vital role Tai Tai would fill in his life and ministry. She later wrote a hilarious poem titled "Ode to Charles," thanking Emily's husband!

Daddy Bill eventually spotted Tai Tai on campus and was told that she had grown up on the mission field in China. He asked her out. For their first date, a performance of Handel's *Messiah*, Tai Tai wore her trusty little black dress along with a string of costume pearls.[1] As God would have it, they fell in love. Daddy Bill met all Tai Tai's qualifications, including blue eyes! They were married on August 13, 1943. Even though they were never missionaries to Tibet, Tai Tai was not disappointed. God had bigger plans, enlisting them to be missionaries to the whole world. Their love affair lasted sixty-three years and surely goes down in the history books as one of the all-time greatest.

Tai Tai and Daddy Bill aren't the only ones in our family who met in a faith-centered setting. My Grampa Lotz, who was raised in a German home in Brooklyn, accepted Christ as a teenager when his German-speaking pastor shared the gospel at church. He felt God's calling in his life to "testify before men." He responded to that call almost immediately and decided to share his testimony at a Sunday night church meeting. It was there, while up front speaking, that he spotted my grandmother sitting on a church pew with her five sisters. He knew right away that she was his future wife. Sure enough, within the year they were married.

They raised four boys together and lost a baby girl in a miscarriage. They didn't have much in terms of worldly possessions, but they loved each other deeply. Gramma's name was Adeline, but Grampa called her Lena. Grampa was a New Yorker right out of central casting: gruff, blunt, plainspoken, but with a great sense of humor. He suffered from diabetes, which resulted in ulcers on the bottom of his feet that Gramma would have to bandage every day. I remember hearing them "argue" in their New York accents. Gramma would say, "Sit still, John!" and Grampa would respond, "Stop it, Lena!" and then they would start laughing. Even though they bickered at times, they genuinely adored each other.

When Dad first laid eyes on Mom, she was seventeen years old and had just graduated from high school. She was busy modeling and planning her future with hopes of attending Wheaton College in the fall. A local boy asked her to go with him to hear a speaker across the valley at the Fellowship of Christian Athletes conference in Black Mountain, North Carolina.

My dad was twenty-eight years old, a former star basketball player at the University of North Carolina who was serving as a captain in the air force at Holloman Air Force Base near Alamogordo, New Mexico. His commanding officer heard about FCA's national camps and told my dad about them. He gave my dad permission to attend the camp in North Carolina.

God's timing was perfect, because Dad was at the FCA conference the night my mom and her date walked in and sat down. My mom's date leaned over to her, pointed to a man several rows ahead, and said, "Hey, that's Danny Lotz. He's the biggest guy here. And he keeps staring at you!" My mom saw the guy her date pointed out but dismissed him because he was obviously a lot older. But Dad said he knew the second he laid eyes on her that he would marry her!

What my mom didn't know was that Daddy Bill had called over to the FCA camp and asked whether they would set my mom up on a date with one of the Christian athletes attending the camp. (I know—it sounded crazy to me too!) Daddy Bill wanted my mom to meet some strong, godly men who were leaders. My dad heard the guys at the camp talking about the opportunity to take my mom on a date. After he saw her, he began to work fervently behind the scenes to be the one chosen.

Mom and Dad had their first date before the week ended; then he returned to the air force base. About a month later, Dad was given leave to fly to North Carolina. He stayed at a boys' summer camp near my mom's home. He took her to dinner, took her canoeing, joined her entire family for dinner, and fell even more deeply in love. My mom wasn't interested, but Tai Tai and Daddy Bill were!

My mom went to California for a leadership institute, and on the way back, she stopped in Denver for Daddy Bill's crusade being held in the stadium there. As it happened, Dad was just getting out of the air force, so he drove up to meet her in Denver. After driving her to Estes Park and showing her the gorgeous Rocky Mountain scenery, he returned her to the hotel. They stopped in the coffee shop, where my mom ordered a chocolate ice cream soda and Dad announced he was in love with her and wanted to marry her. This was their third date! My mom was not impressed and told him so. When he asked whether he could pursue the relationship anyway, she said, "It's a free country. You can do whatever you want."

Later that night, she told Daddy Bill what Danny Lotz had said, fully expecting him to tell her he would handle things and get rid of the guy. Instead, Daddy Bill looked at my mom and said, "I think Danny Lotz is the man you are to marry!" Shortly after that date, my mom was diagnosed with mononucleosis and put on bed rest for months. Her mono was so severe she was unable to attend Wheaton College that fall, which turned into the advantage my dad must have been praying for. It afforded him the opportunity to pursue the relationship.

That fall, he began practicing dentistry in Raleigh. Every weekend, he drove the 250 miles one way to see Mom. Tai Tai had a steak waiting for him when he arrived at the house. Dad would take his supper to my mom's room, eat with her, then leave her alone to rest. But he stayed up late talking and laughing with my grandmother. Tai Tai adored him, and my mom soon agreed. They were engaged on Valentine's Day and married in the fall when my mom was eighteen and my dad was twenty-nine.

They were two drastically different people from different worlds. My dad was as masculine as any man you would ever meet. He once chased a guy, grabbed him by the collar, lifted him up, and scared him half to death for being rude to my mom! My mom was a soft-spoken mountain girl. But they both had unwavering faith, love for God's Word, and love for each other. God blessed their marriage, which lasted forty-nine years, until my dad went to Heaven.

Would you believe that I met my husband on the same porch at the same FCA camp in Black Mountain, North Carolina, where my parents had met twenty-six years earlier? Tai Tai had encouraged me to make a list of the qualities I wanted in the man I would marry. I had prayed as a young teenager that God would protect me from seriously dating anyone except the man I would marry. I had watched my brother and sister go through breakups, and I didn't think my heart could handle that kind of agony.

Steven easily grabbed my attention while attending the same FCA summer camp where my parents met. I couldn't get over how handsome he was. As he was performing in a skit during the evening session, Mom pointed him out to a friend who had heard that I was interested in Steven. When the friend asked which one Steven was, Mom leaned over and said, "He's God"—which was the part he was playing. We were all dying! As embarrassing as this is to write, I actually went back to the cabin my family was staying in and wrote in my journal, "Why can't a guy like Steven Wright notice me?"

A year later, Steven's hopes of playing in the NFL were destroyed after he sustained an injury at the beginning of his fifth year playing football at the University of Central Florida. God then clearly led him to attend Dallas Theological Seminary. As I was starting my junior year at Baylor University in Waco, Texas, he headed to Dallas, where he roomed with my brother, who was on staff at a local church. We attended the same Bible study in Dallas, which is when Steven says he really noticed me.

The fall of my junior year, Steven called my apartment. I about fell out of my chair when I heard his voice! After he asked me out on that first date, we ended up dating for a year and a half, and then he asked me to go up and visit Tai Tai and Daddy Bill after Christmas. Saturday morning we were sitting around with my grandparents, my Uncle Ned, and his wife, Tina. Daddy Bill sat me on his lap, grabbed my left hand, and asked where the ring was. I told him I wasn't engaged. He looked at me like he had let the cat out of the bag! Sure enough, that night, by the living room fire, Steven asked me to marry him. Amazingly, we were sitting on the same couch my parents had been sitting on when my dad had asked my mom for her hand in marriage! We were married that summer at Gaither Chapel in Montreat, North Carolina—the same chapel where my parents and grandparents had been married years before.

God answered my prayer by protecting my heart from having to go through a breakup. He continues to use my marriage to grow my faith, primarily through the difficult times. Thankfully, because I committed to marrying someone who truly loved the Lord, like my grandparents and my parents before me, we have been able to withstand the enemy's attacks on our relationship.

When you are first drawn to the man or woman you can see yourself marrying, the excitement is magical, but if the relationship is not based on Jesus, it can quickly crumble. Both sets of my grandparents, my parents, and Steven and I all met at Christian events—a prayer meeting, a church, and a Fellowship of Christian Athletes camp. I was always taught that the best place to meet a godly man is in a Christian setting.

I spent hours and hours praying for my future spouse. I used to pray that he would have the godly characteristics of men in the Bible. I've done the same with my three girls. I pray on a daily basis, sometimes three or four times a day, for the men they will one day marry. I have taught my daughters to pray in detail for their future spouses, even to the point that they have experienced God putting them (whoever they may be) on their hearts in the middle of the day with a burden to pray for their purity, safety, or stand for the Lord. In a way, my girls are already loving their husbands before they have even met them. They aren't looking for boyfriends in order to just have a date. They want God's best. They want men to ride the river with.

What about you? Have you been praying for your children's future spouses, asking God to lead your children to a campus Bible study, where they might meet godly spouses? Are you raising your children to be the godly men or women that godly men or women will be looking for? Are you teaching them to live the way they want their future spouses to live?

Our careful guidance also can protect our children from a whole lot of dating regret, which comes from dating whoever is available instead of waiting for the right one. In addition, teaching our kids to seek God's plan for marriage is vital to successfully passing the Baton of Truth to future generations.

Ask God to bring His best to your children and grandchildren. Because a love story written in Heaven is worth waiting for!

CREATING
A LEGACY OF WALKING
WITH GOD

Whose future spouse will you pray for?

Be a Jesus Follower: *Teach your children and grandchildren not to settle for less than God's best.*

Isaac brought [Rebekah] into the tent . . . and he married Rebekah. So she became his wife, and he loved her.

Genesis 24:67

I will betroth you to me forever.

Hosea 2:19

22

Facing Death

Just as our marriages can mirror the love of Jesus for His bride and just as our day-to-day interactions with children, grand-children, and others can exemplify God's love and kindness, so, too, our response to life's big events, including death, will proclaim the strength of our faith in the God on whom we rely for every breath. Though goodbyes are never easy, for Jesus Followers the knowledge that our time on earth is short also brings a sense of joy.

My Italian gramma taught me this lesson. She was a hardworking, energetic woman who we thought would live to at least one hundred. She did not have any gray in her glossy brown hair, and her eyes were always filled with joy. I never remember seeing her sad. When she was in her eighties, she once jogged three miles with us on the beach, the picture of health. But not long after that, Grampa hit a telephone pole while he was driving, and Gramma flew through the windshield. She survived, but she never fully mended. After being in the hospital for some time, she went home to recover, only to fall when attempting to climb the stairs with her walker.

My dad traveled to see Gramma in the hospital but eventually returned home because of a busy schedule of patients. He received a phone call early one morning from Gramma, who was still in the hospital. She said, "Daniel, I've seen Jesus! I had a dream where Jesus and I were walking on the beach and He was holding my hand." Then she said, with no small measure of exasperation, "But the nurse came in and woke me up! I told her I didn't want to wake up. I wanted to keep walking with Jesus." The very next day she did exactly that. She went to Heaven!

Despite her physical pain, the reality of death brought Gramma joy because she knew she would be with Jesus. Her words to my dad were indelibly imprinted on my eleven-year-old mind, giving me my first glimpse of what it means to face death with joy. She wasn't afraid to die. She had no doubt that she would close her eyes on this earth and open them in Heaven, because she had placed her faith in Jesus at a young age.

I also learned by watching my grampa face death. His health spiraled down because of diabetes, blindness, and lameness—and he was still grieving the death of Gramma. Every day of the year following Gramma's death, Grampa looked forward to being reunited with her in Heaven. It wasn't a happy year for him because he grieved so deeply. When his health took a turn for the worse, he was placed in a nursing home for most of that last year. We were all heartbroken, knowing how difficult it must have been for him—a New York City street preacher who loved his wife, his ministry, the people of the city, the delicatessens that served his favorite desserts, and the McDonald's that served his favorite morning coffee and biscuit—to be cooped up in a nursing home while being anchored to a strict nutritional diet! But as sad as he was to be without Gramma, he never lost his hope and he never lost sight of his salvation. He knew without a shadow of a doubt that he would see Gramma again in Heaven, because he had placed his faith in Jesus as a young man.

My dad and his brother John flew up to be with Grampa for a few days in the hospital. One morning they left Grampa's side to talk in the hall for a few minutes. The nurse who had been assigned to Grampa had a rich African accent, and from the hallway the brothers heard her singing the hymn "Blessed Assurance." Before she finished, Grampa took his last breath . . . and he was Home. What a way to go!

The nurse later told my dad that Grampa had witnessed to every person who had entered his hospital room. And the way he faced death witnessed to me.

To his final day, Grampa stood firm on the truths of God's Word. Not only did he remember in his hard last year on earth that Jesus lifts up our heads,[1] strengthens our feeble hands and steadies the knees that give way,[2] comforts us when we mourn,[3] draws near to the brokenhearted,[4] and is preparing a place for us,[5] but he also remembered his blessed assurance—"Jesus is mine. Oh, what a foretaste of glory divine!"[6] He showed us that it's possible to face death with peace and anticipation that the best is yet to come.

That blessed assurance is something I've clung to even more tightly since my dad suddenly went to Heaven.

On the day he died, I had been at my parents' house. As Dad walked to the kitchen that morning, I could hear his slow, heavy footsteps and then I saw his head peek around the corner. Even though he was seventy-eight and in miserable health, he was such a kid at heart. When he saw me in the kitchen, his still-sleepy face stretched into a huge smile, and in his deep, broken-muffler voice, he said, "Rach, how ya doin', kid?" I made him oatmeal with fresh blueberries cooked in it. My sweet mom had already laid it out so that all I had to do was stick it in the microwave, but Dad still made a big deal about it as he thanked me.

To help my parents out, I used to clean their house every week, so as Dad ate, I began vacuuming the kitchen. He was bent over the newspaper, reading it with his magnifying glass because he had lost his vision in one eye from a faulty surgery. He was very sweet that morning, like a big, slow-moving teddy bear. He asked me, "Rach, do you want me to move so you can vacuum?" Of course, I said no and thanked him anyway, but I never would have dreamed that would be the last thing he said to me. I wish I could have hugged him, joked with him, or sat down and talked about the Yankees or about the apostle Paul as he loved to do. I wish I could have looked in his eyes, seen the way his face crinkled up when he laughed, or heard him talk about me and my girls, shortening everyone's name. He would call me "Rach," my daughter Sophia was "Soph," and my daughter Riggin was "Rig." My oldest daughter is Bell, so the one-syllable name worked for him.

One of his Bible study guys picked him up for lunch while I was in the back of the house, so I didn't see him leave. I had already returned to my home when he came back and went for a dip in the backyard pool—and the rest is history.

Morrow and I were coaching junior varsity tennis at a Christian school in town, and that afternoon we were on the courts as usual, running practice. Morrow left early, planning to attend a dinner meeting, but she returned soon after and urged me to end practice early. Something about her smile seemed a little funny. I thought maybe something had happened with her husband. She then told me it was Dad. We cleared the courts fast, got into the car, and raced to the hospital. Even as she filled me in, my phone began blowing up with text messages from people who had seen news videos taken from helicopters of my dad being pulled out of the pool by EMS.

The next three days were a blur. We kept Dad on life support in the hope that he would respond or wake up, but he had already gone home to Heaven. When we finally removed life support, Mom, Morrow and Traynor, Jonathan and Jenny, and Steven and I were all in the room. My mom led us in a hymn, and then she read passages of Scripture about Heaven. I was crying my eyes out and asking Dad not to leave us. It was like I was a young child all over again. I didn't want him to go.

Facing the death of a loved one is devastating, and I won't pretend otherwise. But I want to tell you how my dad had prepared me for that moment.

For years Dad would say things like "This is it. I don't think I'll make it another year, Rach!" . . . "Rach, when I'm gone, just toss me in a pine box and drop me in the ground. I won't be there. I'll be in Heaven!" . . . "Rach, this is just a tent. When I die, I'll be with Jesus!" . . . "Rach, do you think you'll say some nice things about me when I die?" He would also ask, "Rach, do you think anyone will come to my funeral?" and then laugh. He would talk about his funeral as if it would be the event of the year (which it turned out to be). I think he wanted to attend it himself! He made talking about his death as natural as drinking water. He joked about it and talked about it so much that it actually helped me. He wasn't the least bit afraid of death, and he certainly never dreaded it. He faced death with gusto. Nothing in this life held him back. He never cared about money or things or status or fame. He just wanted to finish his race well.

Three years after Dad went to Heaven, Daddy Bill followed. He was ninety-nine, but I still wasn't ready for him to go. As I look at how the world has plummeted morally and turned so violent since his death, I'm thankful he isn't here to see it, though part of me wishes he were here to speak wisdom from the platform God gave him.

Yet I know that Daddy Bill greatly anticipated Heaven. He longed to be free from his "earthly tent."[7] He was more than ready to go. He had been telling people his whole life how to get to Heaven, how to have their sins forgiven, how to be assured that one day they would be face to face with Jesus and live with Him for all eternity. Now he was ready to experience death himself. He was never afraid to die; he never worried about dying; he never doubted where he would go when he died; he was steady in his love for, commitment to, and faith in Jesus to the very end!

Daddy Bill beautifully showed me that when I am facing death, I can have genuine peace. God was with him as he preached to millions all around the world, and God was with him at home, in his bed, until his last breath.

Literally not a day goes by when I don't talk about my dad or say something he would have said. I miss him and my grandparents—achingly so—but I have absolutely no doubt that I will see them again in Heaven. That's the jump-up-and-down, mind-blowing, over-the-top, indescribable blessing that Jesus Followers have! We get to go to Heaven for all eternity and be with our loved ones that have also placed their faith in Jesus. Facing death can be joyous with Jesus!

For those left behind, grief is all too real. However, as Jesus Followers, we don't grieve without hope.[8]

This chapter has been the hardest one for me to write, because I so miss my loved ones. But it's almost as though they've gone on a long trip. I know I'll see them again. With that very real hope, I find myself thinking about what they're doing in Heaven. I imagine what it will be like when my dad and my grandparents see my girls grown. I try to think of what I'll cook for dinner when we all sit around the table with Jesus. I imagine what it's like to serve and work without any hindrances or sin.

Heaven is as real as the chair I'm sitting in right now. It's a sure thing for Jesus Followers, and it's something I long for every day as I praise God for the place He's preparing for me and for my family.

CREATING A LEGACY OF WALKING WITH GOD

Make a list of the things you most look forward to about Heaven.

Be a Jesus Follower: *Keep looking up!*

Do not let your hearts be troubled. Trust in God; trust also in me. In my Father's house are many rooms; if it were not so, I would have told you. I am going there to prepare a place for you. And if I go and prepare a place for you, I will come back and take you to be with me that you also may be where I am.

John 14:1–3

PART FOUR

Our Work

By faith Noah, when warned about things not yet seen,
in holy fear built an ark to save his family.

Hebrews 11:7

noch received the Baton of Truth, grasped it firmly as he walked with God, then passed the Baton to his son Methuselah, who passed it to his son Lamech, who passed it to his son Noah. Noah received the Baton, and, praise God, not only did he witness, worship, and walk with God; he also worked for God.

Have you ever stopped to think about what would have happened had Noah been too busy, too tired, too apathetic, or too self-absorbed to work for God? Without his work, you and I wouldn't be here today! His work for God is of legendary proportions. Even those unfamiliar with the rest of the Bible know about Noah and his work.

The Work Needs Motivation

What motivated Noah to work for God? I wonder whether it was his father's prayers. When Noah was born, Lamech expressed his deep desire that his son would "comfort us in the labor and painful toil of our hands caused by the ground the LORD has cursed."[1] Lamech must have been a man of prayer. Reading into his words slightly, it seems that he was praying that Noah's life would not be wasted, that it would count for God. In other words, using our metaphor of the relay race, he seems to have been praying that his son would receive and relay the Baton of Truth.

When do you pray for your children? When do you pray for your grandchildren? When do you pray for your nieces and nephews and the other children who God brings across your path? If you are not praying for them, who is? And how should you and I pray for them? Let's pray for their salvation first of all. Pray that they would grow up to be Jesus Followers. Pray for their wisdom. Their friends. Their choice of studies. Their future spouses. As I pass people in the mall, sit by them on a plane, or watch them jog down the street, I wonder who is praying for them. How tragic to think that there are people all around us, young and old, for whom no one is praying. While we can't pray for everyone, you and I can at least pray for those in our families and those who cross our paths.

As businesses began to reopen after the initial COVID-19 lockdown, I met a friend for lunch in a local restaurant. We couldn't help but plunge into a conversation about the national unrest in the wake of George Floyd's horrific murder. In a few moments, we were served by a young African American man. After he left to turn in our order, we bowed our heads, and my friend asked God's blessing on our meal. When she lifted her head, I blurted out regretfully that we should have asked the server whether we could pray for him. When he returned with our drink order, I told him we had just prayed and I wanted to know whether we could pray for him in any way. He immediately gave us a request, then held out his hands, bowed his head, and waited for us to pray! We took his hands, and I prayed as he had asked. When I concluded the prayer, his eyes were filled with tears. He said that he was trying hard not to cry, that we had no idea all he was going through at that time. And he thanked us. For praying. Such a simple act that meant so much to all of us.

Lamech's prayers seem to have motivated Noah to walk with God and to work for God when no one else did. And I wonder whether Noah also drew motivation and inspiration from his godly heritage—those spiritual giants in the nine previous generations.

As Rachel-Ruth noted earlier, my husband's father was a pastor from New York City who, along with his wife, raised four sons. All of his sons were aware of whose they were. Because they were raised in the church, they were identified with the Lord Jesus, but they were also identified as the sons of John Lotz. That strong sense of belonging was passed down not only to the four brothers but also to their eleven children and then to their grandchildren. It's remarkable! Every member of the Lotz family has received the Baton, is carrying it as he or she runs the race, and is passing it securely to those around them. My father-in-law taught me the value of impressing on our children a strong sense of belonging to a godly family.

The Work Requires Perseverance

Whatever Noah's motivation may have been, we know that he walked with God and he worked for God. The two spiritual disciplines are closely intertwined. It was as Noah walked with God that he learned what was on God's mind—and it was judgment: "The LORD saw how great man's wickedness on the earth had become, and that every inclination of the thoughts of his heart was only evil all the time. The LORD was grieved that he had made man on the earth, and his heart was filled with pain. So the LORD said, 'I will wipe mankind, whom I have created, from the face of the earth.'"[2]

God's word must have been terrifying to Noah. He knew the civilization in which he lived was wicked—blasphemous, obscene, idolatrous, and demonic. But I wonder whether he had realized just how saturated in sin the human race had become. When had it passed the point of no return?

Before Noah could process the jumble of thoughts that must have exploded in his mind, God continued to speak: "I am going to put an end to all people, for the earth is filled with violence because of them. I am surely going to destroy both them and the earth. So make yourself an ark."[3]

As Noah walked with God, he learned that not only judgment but also salvation was on God's mind. The impending judgment would fall on the entire world, but in His mercy, God wanted to offer salvation to those who would accept it. He told Noah to build an ark. And Noah did exactly what God told him to do.[4]

Think about it. How could one man have taken on such a massive job? I expect his sons helped when they were old enough, but until then, did Noah have to hire day laborers to help? And where would he get the money to pay them? How would he gather all the materials necessary? While we don't know some of these answers, we do know it took Noah more than 120 years to build the ark! Talk about persevering in the work! And with no encouragement from his friends and neighbors.

What courage it must have taken for Noah to do God's work in front of the whole wicked world. The people living around him must have laughed at what they considered an old man on the brink of lunacy. No one had ever seen rain at that stage of human history, no one had ever seen a big body of water, no one had ever seen a boat, no one had ever even seen a building the size of the ark, and no one had ever seen that many animals gathered in one place! I wonder whether Noah's friends and neighbors considered his work to be a spectacle for their entertainment. Was he the object of their scorn and the butt of their rude jokes? Did they ostracize his family?

Added to what was surely a barrage of criticism would have been persecution. The New Testament tells us that Noah was a preacher of righteousness.[5] I wonder if he stood in the door of the ark, warning people that judgment was coming? Did he passionately . . . desperately . . . cry out as he offered them salvation from judgment by inviting them into the safety of the ark? Apparently no one listened or took his preaching seriously. And no one—no one!—believed judgment was coming.

The Work Points Others to Salvation

In the end, of course, Noah and his family entered the ark, God shut the door, and the judgment no one thought was coming, came! Outside the ark "every living thing that moved on the face of the earth perished." And "everything on dry land that had the breath of life in its nostrils died. Every living thing on the face of the earth was wiped out."[6] But the ark that God had told Noah to build was the very means of saving him and his family. Without a doubt, as Noah heard the water crashing outside and the screams of those who were dying, he must have been overwhelmed with gratitude that he had made time to walk with God so that he wasn't caught by surprise. As God had revealed what was on His mind, Noah was not only forewarned but also had clear instructions. He knew how to prepare. He knew what his specific work was, and he persevered until the work was finished.

I walk with God too. While I don't walk as closely or consistently as I would like, I do walk with Him every day, and I can say with certainty that judgment is on the mind of God. He would be less than His holy, perfect self if He didn't judge this blasphemous, obscene, rebellious world in which we are living. Yet while God is certainly just and righteous, He is also patient. He is not willing for any to perish but wants all to come to repentance.[7] Which is why I'm confident that salvation from judgment is also on His mind. Jesus explained, "God so loved the world that he gave his one and only Son, that whoever believes in him shall not perish [come under judgment] but have eternal life [salvation]."[8]

So let's get to work! God has provided an ark, a refuge from the storm of His judgment. But the people all around us don't know that judgment is coming, and they therefore don't know that salvation from judgment is even necessary. We need to warn them. If from time to time it occurs to them that they will be held accountable for their willful wickedness, they don't know how to be saved. Our work is to let people know that, yes, judgment is coming, but God offers salvation from His judgment. Just as there was only one door into Noah's ark, there is only one way into salvation from God's judgment: through the cross of Jesus Christ. Our work is to tell people about Jesus, to pass the Baton of Truth to everyone willing to grab hold and run with it.

Noah worked for God, and as a result, you and I are here today. What if Noah had had a different attitude? *Well, You know, God, I don't need to work for You. Just look at who my father is. My father's Lamech; my grandfather's Methuselah. I can trace my godly heritage all the way back to Enoch and Enosh and Seth and Adam himself. I can just ride in on their coattails.* Or what if he had rationalized his way out of building the ark? *Oh my goodness, I could never pray like Lamech, walk like Enoch, worship like Enosh, or witness like Abel. So I won't even try. I'll just curl up in a ball and hide from the world around me.* Or what if he had cowered in fear and kept a low profile, trying to blend in with those around him so he wouldn't risk rejection and persecution?

Have you been making excuses for not working for God? For not passing the Baton? For not sharing the gospel? For not naming the name of Jesus and explaining that He is the only Savior from the judgment that's coming? There is no other name by which anyone can be saved.[9] He is the only way to the Father.[10] But how will people know if you and I don't tell them? Who would be saved if we would get to work? Like Noah, could it be those in our own families?

Ask God to give you an assignment. A work to do. Start a neighborhood Bible study. Teach Sunday school. Facilitate a small group in your church. Maybe it's simply the work of your profession: being a healthcare worker, a teacher, an attorney, a soccer mom, a coach, a business professional, a truck driver, a _____ (put your profession in the blank)—not just for the purpose of making a living but for the purpose of making Jesus known. Showing those around you what Jesus would be like if He were working in your profession. Revealing Him in such a way that others are drawn into the ark of salvation by your example.

Don't be afraid to let others know you are working for Jesus. Don't be afraid that if you tell others about Him, even those within your own home, you will be criticized. Ostracized. Ridiculed. If you are, so be it! Don't let fear keep you from being faithful to run your race with perseverance while you pass the Baton to others. The salvation of those closest to you may depend on it.

Accept the Baton of Truth that Rachel-Ruth is passing to you through the following stories, and ask God to use them to encourage and motivate you to work for Him.

23

The World Awaits

How are you expanding your children's worldview? Would you be willing to let your child go on a mission trip to open his or her eyes to a needy world?

One critical aspect of passing the Baton of Truth to the next generation is to give our children firsthand experiences of the impact truth makes in the lives of those in another culture or those who are less fortunate. My great-grandparents were medical missionaries to China, my great-aunt was a missionary to Korea, my grandparents were missionaries to the whole world, so I grew up with a global perspective. While I strive to nurture that worldview in my kids, I also want to teach them to notice the needs of those around them, whether in their classrooms, in our neighborhood, or across town.

My parents intentionally directed our attention beyond ourselves to nurture in us a compassion that mirrors God's love for people. While I was in high school, I began to feel a stirring in my heart for Africa. The burden really grew, as I described earlier, when I traveled with my mom on one of her speaking trips to South Africa. I observed, listened, and absorbed everything! Witnessing the devastating poverty in some areas of the country, seeing the vast and beautifully rugged land, and getting to know the people left an indelible mark on my heart. I'll never forget meeting believers there who were striving to know God in a personal way, drinking in every word that the Lord gave my mom to share as she spoke throughout the country. I fell in love with Africa! I told Mom that I hoped I would be able to return one day, and I began praying that I would.

God opened that door for me the summer after my sophomore year in college. My Uncle Franklin asked whether I would like to go to Rwanda for the summer, along with his son Will and another cousin, Noelle, to help out in the orphanages run by Samaritan's Purse.

Less than a year earlier, Rwanda had endured a catastrophic genocide in which one tribe tried to annihilate the other, causing the murder of over one million people in one hundred days. The tragedy shocked the world and gave us an unwanted glimpse into the dark depths of the human heart. A hauntingly memorable quote from a missionary was splashed across the cover of *Time* magazine, accompanied by a picture of a stricken Rwandan refugee holding her baby: "There are no devils left in Hell. . . . They are all in Rwanda."[1]

The firsthand stories that I heard underscored the horrors that provoked the statement. During my six weeks in Rwanda, I heard countless gut-wrenching examples of inhumanity. People were herded like cattle onto a bridge and attacked with machetes until they jumped to their deaths in the shallow water below. I was told that their bodies piled high and the water turned blood red. Right up the road from that bridge was a church to which Rwandans had fled. When the building was packed with people, someone locked the doors and set it on fire. The yard of the compound where we stayed contained a mass burial site, and the outer walls were still marked with bloodstains. I heard of children being forced to commit murders, and I saw countless people who were maimed, missing arms and legs. One of the orphans we had the privilege of ministering to had half her face blown away by a gunshot. As we drove around and interacted with people, it was impossible not to notice that many were covered in scars from machete wounds. While the scars were evidence of miraculous survival, they also spoke of traumatic horror. This was a desperate place with desperate people who desperately needed someone to tell them of the hope to be found in Jesus.

Samaritan's Purse was the first relief organization to arrive after the genocide. It provided aid on multiple levels, including setting up orphanages all over the country to house and care for the many children whose parents either had been murdered or had fled to neighboring countries. The Lord had given me the high honor of working in those orphanages, loving on the children of Rwanda and sharing Jesus with them.

When my plane approached what was left of the airport in Kigali, Rwanda, my mouth hung open and my heart started to pound. The windows of the tiny, run-down airport building had been shot out, and bullet holes riddled the outer walls. When the plane stopped, I stood to retrieve my bags and was shocked to find that I was the only person getting off the plane! Everyone else stayed put and looked at me like I had lost my mind. They were on their way to Kenya, most probably planning to vacation at one of the many safari resorts. And here I was, stepping off a plane into utter despair. But I felt beyond blessed by the privilege of serving these people who were created in God's image, just like me.

My cousins Will and Noelle met me at the airport. I saw Will and his familiar grin through the plexiglass window as I stood before soldiers that were approximately my age or possibly even younger. They were pointing machine guns at me while motioning to the open suitcase that another of Uncle Franklin's ministries, World Medical Mission, had asked me to bring. What I hadn't realized was that the suitcase was packed with a plethora of medical supplies: needles, syringes, scissors, and even knives. I began to sweat profusely when the soldiers opened the luggage and seemed to want an explanation. Since I didn't speak Kinyarwanda, I tried to find a way to convey that this was for a medical organization, to help people. They looked at me with confusion and concern. The situation wasn't good, and after a long international flight, it wasn't easy to think straight, especially with my ADHD, not to mention the semiautomatic weapons pointed at me! Finally I said, "Samaritan's Purse." Their faces lit up, and they let me proceed. It was my first glimpse of how respected Samaritan's Purse was in their country.

Despite the crazy welcome, I couldn't have been more thrilled to be there. I spent most of the next six weeks working in orphanages. Part of the time, I worked in the hospital, inventorying supplies. No matter where I served, every day I was awed by one main lesson: how deep the love of Jesus was for every person. I saw God's love for the Rwandan people evidenced by the involvement of Samaritan's Purse in establishing orphanages and setting up and equipping hospitals. I saw the love of God in pastors who retained their joy as they shepherded their people on a path to forgiveness and reconciliation. I saw the love of God in the exuberance and resilience of the children who were satisfied with one crayon and a game of leapfrog. Not one person in the entire world escapes God's full and compassionate attention. I knew He was there!

Noelle and I spent day after day holding and hugging babies and toddlers that God had created and protected through the awful days of the genocide. The faces of tiny boys and girls would light up when we rounded the corner to enter the small dirt yard of the orphanage. I sometimes had up to six toddlers trying to sit in my lap or climb on my back, wanting nothing but affection and love from anyone who would stop to hold them. My heart breaks even now just thinking about them. I've often wondered where they are and what they're doing. Their precious faces are forever implanted in my mind. I still pray for them.

We spent hours playing with the school-aged children and trying our best to teach them games through interpretation. The interpreter would sometimes misunderstand a critical part of the game, and the kids would end up hopping instead of running or squatting instead of standing. It was very comical. One of the funniest sights was trying to teach them how to play leapfrog! They, of course, thought we had lost our minds and laughed so hard they had tears in their eyes.

We performed puppet shows depicting stories in the Bible. We taught them crafts and basically did whatever we could to bring smiles to their faces and let them know how much Jesus loved them. The people we came in contact with were thirsty for Jesus and appreciative that we had come. But like with most mission trips, I was the one who was ministered to. I was and still am truly humbled at how eager the children were to learn. They were always ready to laugh, despite their surroundings.

When I headed home to America, I found that it wasn't easy to get reacclimated. I had been forever affected by what I had experienced. I had a hard time even walking into grocery stores, a little sickened at how much we had available to us. Having clean, easily accessible water to drink from the faucet or to brush my teeth—without boiling it first—seemed luxurious. And going to bed in an air-conditioned house, with clean sheets and a roof over my head, were things that I began to see in a new light. My perspective on what matters had shifted. My worldview had expanded infinitely, putting a spotlight on the blessings I had previously taken for granted as well as making me keenly aware of the greed and self-centeredness in my life, qualities that seem to come naturally to most American youth.

I am thankful to my parents and grandparents for raising me to know that not everyone has a roof over his or her head at night, not everyone has food to eat, not everyone has the privileges that we have in America. As we were growing up, our priorities didn't revolve around us, our feelings, or our small problems. Jesus was at the forefront of everything.

My parents often hosted missionaries, ministry workers, and other Christian friends in our home for dinner. They wisely had me sit and listen to countless conversations about what the Lord was doing all over the world. Starting back in high school, my mom took me on many of her international trips—to Europe, Australia, the Middle East, and Africa—opening my eyes to more than just the bubble of life in Raleigh. Daddy Bill and Tai Tai were constantly expanding my perspective with stories of their ministry around the world. And Grampa and Gramma inspired us through describing the ways they were ministering to people in the most underresourced neighborhoods of the Bronx.

My dad wasn't a world traveler and didn't enjoy being in unfamiliar territory, but he made sure that I read biographies of missionaries and other outstanding men and women of faith such as David Livingstone, Corrie ten Boom, Hudson Taylor, Gladys Aylward, Amy Carmichael, and Jim Elliot. My girls haven't had the opportunity to travel around the world, but I've made sure that they've read these same biographies to broaden their horizons.

While the ministry calling of my parents and grandparents provided a unique lens on the world, I'm convinced of the importance of expanding the worldview of all children so that they don't become focused on material things and consumed with themselves. Social media platforms like Instagram, TikTok, and Snapchat promote narcissistic behavior and foster anxiety and depression. Sending kids on mission trips, telling them missionary stories, or taking them to serve at a local soup kitchen or hospital will open their eyes to a world bigger than themselves, a world that needs Jesus. I believe it will cause them to be more thankful, more compassionate, and less self-centered.

For seven years, I taught a missions chapel at a local Christian school, sharing missionary stories that I had heard or read about. Many times I would bring in missionaries and interview them in front of the kids so that they could hear firsthand what the Lord was doing around the world. Many children put their faith in Jesus just through hearing those stories.

As you and I seek to participate in the work of God, we can look for local opportunities to teach our kids the importance of being focused on others. Collect toys and clothes that you could give to needy children in your area. Participate in Operation Christmas Child, which sends thousands of gift-filled shoeboxes to little children all around the world, including Rwanda. Look through the Christmas gift catalog of Samaritan's Purse, and let your child help pick out a gift for an underprivileged person. Sponsor a child through

Compassion International, and give your kids the responsibility of corresponding with him or her, learning from their pen pal even as together you offer help and encouragement.

So many needs are all around us. There are people who are help-less and homeless and hurting, people who are sick and suffering and struggling, people who are abused and afraid and alone. There are so many needs that I can feel overwhelmed, tempted to throw up my hands and exclaim, "What can I do?" But then I bow my head and ask God to bring to my attention the specific needs He wants me to get involved in meeting. Would you do the same?

Who knows? When our children are grown, we may discover that what seemed to be a small effort to open their eyes and hearts to a needy world had a long-lasting impact. They may look back and say that the highlight of their upbringing was not the beach vacation, the trip to Disney World, the new cell phone, or even the school honors they received for their hard-earned grades. I wonder whether they will say that the highlight was the times we responded to the needs of others together.

CREATING
A LEGACY OF WORKING
FOR GOD

Pray that God would give you a heart of compassion and open your eyes to the needs He wants you and your family to meet.

Be a Jesus Follower: *Look around. Help someone.*

The King will reply, "I tell you the truth, whatever you did for one of the least of these brothers of mine, you did for me."

Matthew 25:40

He said to them, "Go into all the world and preach the good news to all creation."

Mark 16:15

24

Hard Work

On typical Saturday mornings in the fall and winter, my dad would have me out in the yard doing chores. His archnemesis was the pine tree, and we had a bazillion of them in our yard. I can still smell the pine straw and hear his rake pulling at the pine needles that had laid claim to the ground, covering the grass. He always used the big, heavy rake that seemed to tear out the grass along with the pine needles, but I think he hated pine needles so much that it was worth the sacrifice of a few blades of grass. He'd hand me the light-weight rake and assign me a section of the yard. I would end up with a sore back and some blisters on my hands, but working hard to clear out the pine needles gave me a sense of accomplishment.

Years later, after my dad went to Heaven, I gasped when I first visited his gravesite. Right next to his plot stood a big old pine tree, dropping pine cones and pine needles all over. Even as we all stood there, a pine needle fell and nailed me in the head like a carefully aimed missile. I just knew it had to be Dad's angel causing us to laugh when we were so incredibly sad.

While hard work seemed to come naturally to my dad, I think

it actually was ingrained in him from an early age. My dad was not raised to sit around. He was born in 1937, into a generation that knew war, knew what it was to ration food, knew how to stretch a dollar, and knew that everyone, young and old, had to work hard in order to keep a household running. His was not a generation raised on social media and television but one instilled with grit and determination, a generation with the backbone to work thirty years in one job whether or not they liked it. And if they lost a job, they would immediately find whatever work they could to provide for their families.

We mimic so much of what we see exemplified by our parents. I know my dad's work ethic was a reflection of his own parents, who worked hard their entire lives. My grampa was a second-generation German American who served as a preacher in different Baptist churches in and around New York City. He donated his salary back to the church, so he made a living by working for the New York Telephone Company during the week, then prepared his sermons after work.

My gramma was a second-generation Italian American, one of twelve siblings. Starting back in the late 1920s, an era when it was less common for married women to hold jobs, she was a dental hygienist on Fifth Avenue in New York City. She worked all day and then took the subway home in time to cook dinner for Grampa and their four boys. She also kept a large vegetable garden in their backyard in Northport, Long Island. She helped in the church and sang in the choir, doing what she could to support my grandfather. When they came to visit us, I never remember seeing Gramma sit around. In fact, I will never forget getting up on a couple of mornings and seeing her in her bra and underwear, scrubbing the bricks out on our front patio! I guess she was hot and saw no sense in dirtying clothes. My mom put a stop to that—graciously.

When my dad was eight years old, Grampa moved the family to Falls, Pennsylvania, while he commuted to seminary for four years. Dad and his three brothers worked the farm that my gramma's family owned, and then they took the produce to the market. I was told that my gramma's Italian mother made her own pasta and hung it on the farmhouse porch with clothespins to dry it.

After four years in Pennsylvania, Grampa moved the family back to Long Island, where my dad and his brothers went to school, played basketball, and worked in potato fields. My dad and his brother John even got their picture in the Long Island paper, with a caption misstating that they were immigrant boys toiling in the fields. His parents had him doing hard manual labor from a young age, which instilled in him a strong drive to stay active and push himself to get things done.

In high school, Dad worked in a bowling alley at night, setting up bowling pins. He said it was tough work because he had to move quickly from lane to lane, setting up the pins so that people could bowl. In college, he waited tables. He would get back to the dorm late, study, and get about three hours of sleep, then get up and go to class. He also dug ditches for the highway, which was his least favorite job. In the summers, my dad delivered Pepsi-Cola on Long Island. Guys back then didn't normally lift weights, but Dad earned his strength by unloading huge cases of Pepsi, most of which had to be carried down a flight of wooden steps to the basement of whatever restaurant or bar he was delivering to.

While I was growing up, my dad was always in motion. If he wasn't drilling people's teeth, then he was at home working in the yard or playing basketball or tennis until the sun went down. He never wanted to be idle. Just about every Sunday afternoon, he invited a bunch of guys to come over and play basketball in our backyard. Each of those guys respected him for the athlete that he was and were also influenced by his godly example. Every Thursday night for years, he drove thirty minutes to Chapel Hill, where he helped lead the Fellowship of Christian Athletes meeting for the university students. His annual Christmas gift to each of the pastors at our church was a truckload of firewood that he purchased from our neighbor who chopped wood as a side job. Dad would load it up, deliver it to each pastor's house, and then unload it for him. It wasn't until my dad was in his seventies—suffering from debilitating diabetes, neuropathy in his feet, dialysis three times a week, heart problems, and blindness in one eye—that I saw him forced to slow down because of his lack of mobility.

My dad worked hard but always wanted to focus on the Lord. One way he accomplished this was by teaching Sunday school every weekend as long as I can remember. Mom still has drawers full of his yellow legal pads on which he wrote his lessons late at night.

People always knew they could count on my dad when they needed a helping hand. He was an active part of the body of Christ and was an example to everyone of Christlike service. Dad urged everyone to be a doer. He taught me not to be lazy, to jump up when I was asked to do something, not to delegate when it was something I could do, to look for ways to help, and never to shy away from hard work. He loved using his hands, and he set a great example for us. I want to set that kind of example for my children.

When young people today are quick to help out without complaining, adults definitely take notice. And our kids notice and absorb our attitude toward work. Being hardworking Jesus Followers means we aren't shrinking back from difficult assignments, we aren't asking for handouts, we have a sense of fulfillment when we do a job well, and people don't hear us complaining.

Will the example you're setting for your kids and grandkids help or hinder their work ethic? It's a challenge because of all the distractions caused by the technology at our kids' fingertips. They live so much in the virtual world that it's up to us as parents to bring them back to the present by teaching them hard work, giving them tasks that make them use their muscles, and showing them how to stay active.

To be candid, I don't do a great job involving my kids in work, because I don't like to delegate. So often it just seems easier to do things myself. But I am trying to encourage my girls to be hard workers, whether it's by setting the table, vacuuming the house, changing the litter box, giving 100 percent effort in their sports, or even carrying the bag of balls at practice. As little as these things are, I believe they will establish a strong work ethic, building the habit of seeking opportunities to honor God by serving others. Plus, one day their spouses will thank me.

CREATING A LEGACY OF WORKING FOR GOD

How can you—and your family—use your God-given skills and energy to cheerfully tackle a project, whether in your home, in your neighborhood, at your church, or elsewhere?

Be a Jesus Follower: *Do something.*

Whatever your hand finds to do, do it with all your might, for in the grave, where you are going, there is neither working nor planning nor knowledge nor wisdom.

Ecclesiastes 9:10

25

Full Attention

Along with working to meet the practical and spiritual needs of others, as Jesus Followers we are called to demonstrate love and kindness in our closest relationships.

When I was a little girl, I remember crawling under our wooden coffee table that was made out of an old ship door. I would nestle my pillow on one of the wide, stubby legs of the table and lie down on our green shag carpet. With my polyester nightgown tucked around me and fuzzy socks covering my fast-growing feet, I would fix my eyes on the console television set, which was topped with a doily and a lamp. My mom or dad would turn the knob on the television to get it to the right channel, and then we weren't allowed to talk. This wasn't *The A-Team* or *The Cosby Show* or even Carolina basketball, all of which were frequently viewed at our house. It was the Billy Graham Crusade television special.

No matter where the crusade was being held, whether I was present in the stadium or watching it stream across the airwaves, I always felt God's presence and love. I remember singing along with Uncle Cliff Barrows as he led the tens of thousands of people attending the crusade as if we were in church, vigorously directing each note with his huge choir behind him bellowing the hymns. He led with such passion. The love of Jesus could be clearly seen on his face. Uncle Bev Shea was the same way. I always saw kindness in his eyes, especially when he sang. His warm baritone voice settled and prepared our hearts before my grandfather gave his message.

As much as I loved all the testimonies and music that began a crusade, what I really looked forward to was getting a glimpse of Daddy Bill, if only for a few minutes. Looking back, I am so thankful he upheld God's Word, repeating again and again in each sermon, "The Bible says . . ." He had an undeniable heart for preaching the gospel with passion and conviction. His messages were easy to pay attention to, even for a hyper little kid. I saw how God used him to give out His truth clearly and powerfully but with a humble heart. When the invitation was given and the hymn "Just as I Am" began to play, I always got choked up watching people stream forward to place their faith in Jesus. At the end of the program, I would mouth the familiar addresses Daddy Bill gave viewers who wanted to write to the ministry: "Just write to Billy Graham. Minneapolis, Minnesota. That's all the address you need. Or if you are in Canada, write to Billy Graham, Winnipeg, Manitoba." Then I would look for my Uncle Ted's name in the credits, because he was the producer of the program, before sleepily making my way upstairs to bed.

Throughout my life, people have asked me, "What's it like having a famous grandfather?" I don't really know how to answer because I have never known anything different. My grandfather may have traveled and preached all over the world, he may have had numerous audiences with dignitaries and kings, he may have been friends with celebrities and had a direct line to presidents, he may have preached behind the Iron Curtain and been the voice that everyone turned to in crisis, and he may have had those hour-long television specials that thousands watched around the world, but to me he was just Daddy Bill. I loved to smell his clean, Coppertone scent and put my head on his soft sweater as I hugged him, hold his hand while we talked, or listen to his deep voice as he conversed with whoever was in the room. I love my memories of playing on his front lawn while he, my mom, and Tai Tai sat in the sun. We kids would chase the dogs around the yard and attempt to dodge the ever-present wasps that nested in the shingles on the roof, sip on iced tea with lemonade, and rock in the rocking chairs underneath the wisteria that crowned the porch with flowers and bees.

Even though Daddy Bill was something of a celebrity, I knew him as a very grandfatherly grandfather. He often took afternoon walks with us down the long mountain driveway. He always wore soft blue jeans with a baseball cap and a denim jacket if it was chilly. We searched for snake skins left behind in the crevices of the rock wall that held up the steep embankment. We talked about the dogs that would chase absolutely anything we threw. We sat on a bench and looked out over the Blue Ridge Mountains through the trees. We listened to his stories of apples being stored in the old cellar on the side of the mountain or swimming in the cold stream-fed mountain pool or hiking up to the old Bear's Den. Sometimes he leaned on a walking stick, and sometimes he just held our hands as we walked.

As Daddy Bill got older and less mobile, my mom, Morrow, my girls, and I would sit in his room as he ate breakfast. He loved a hearty breakfast of eggs, bacon, oatmeal, toast, hot coffee, and a banana that he would peel by breaking it in half. He'd toss some of his bacon to the dogs and cat because he loved the fact that they looked forward to it every morning, waiting patiently in front of him for their special treat. At our evening meals, Daddy Bill told us stories of his travels—but only when we asked him to. He never bragged. Ever. He was attentive to us and asked us questions. He loved hearing about what God was doing in our lives. He wanted to know what I was teaching in Bible study and what my girls were involved in. When we were with him, he was fully invested in us. He always managed to make us feel special.

Daddy Bill exuded a real-life Cary Grant type of elegance but with southern charm. He was kind, thoughtful, and attentive. With all that he had going on and with all the people who wanted his ear, he had a remarkable way of giving you his full attention. I felt loved and cherished when I was around him.

On one occasion when Daddy Bill was mostly bedridden, my mom, Morrow and her husband, my girls, Steven, and I all sat around him. My youngest daughter, Riggin, who is very confident and talkative, was seven years old at the time. She asked Daddy Bill question after question after question. She asked what his favorite animal was. He thought and then said it was a rabbit. She excitedly responded, "Me too!" She asked what his favorite color was. "Blue." What was his favorite place he ever visited? "India." He seemed to thoroughly enjoy her interrogation. And on and on it went, until finally she whispered to him, "I have to go to the potty." He answered in a preaching voice, "Then you'd better go!" We all cracked up! That evening is one of my dearest memories. He loved Riggin. He had such a connection with her, as he did with all his grandchildren. He never dismissed my girls and never thought of them as a nuisance. So even though my grandfather was not present as often as other grandfathers may be, he made the most of his time with us by giving us his full attention when we were together.

As I reflect on Daddy Bill's example, I glimpse my heavenly Father, whose eyes "are on the righteous and [whose] ears are attentive to their prayer."[1] While I know Daddy Bill was very busy, he doesn't compare to my heavenly Father, who is Lord of the universe, who has planets to spin, history to direct, people to save, prayers to answer, and a million other things to do yet gives you and me His full attention. He longs to hear what we have to say.

Why do I fail so many times at giving my family or my friends my full attention when they are speaking or sharing their time with me? Yes, we live in a world of constant distractions with cell phones and email and work and entertainment, but the moments that we invest in our relationships with people not only bless us but also bless those around us. To give others our focused attention conveys that we truly want to know them, to feel connected to them as we value, understand, and love them. When my grandfather gave me his full attention, he taught me that while work is necessary, even a grandchild is more important.

What a lesson for me to remember. As a busy parent and future grandparent, I want to make my children and grandchildren feel loved and cherished by giving them my full attention when I am with them. I want my girls to know that I want to hear what they have to say, just as Daddy Bill did with me.

CREATING A LEGACY OF WORKING FOR GOD

Ask God to open your eyes to opportunities to make the people in your life feel valued, heard, and loved.

Be a Jesus Follower: *Listen with your ears and eyes.*

Those who feared the LORD talked with each other, and the LORD listened and heard. A scroll of remembrance was written in his presence concerning those who feared the LORD and honored his name. "They will be mine," says the LORD Almighty, "in the day when I make up my treasured possession."

Malachi 3:16–17

26

Managing Expectations

I would never want to give the impression that anyone in my family is perfect. As much as I value the principles exemplified by my parents and grandparents, sometimes those principles came in the wake of difficult misunderstandings or even mistakes that had to be remedied. This is clearly illustrated by the struggle I had with math, which triggered my dad's struggle with me.

I never ever have been good with numbers. I still break out in a sweat just remembering timed math tests in elementary school. Some kids in the class would be out of their chairs, bent over their tests, frantically racing the clock to finish their times table before everyone else. The fact that I noticed what they were doing shows that I wasn't even looking at my paper. I could feel the stress in the room, and the numbers on my test, along with numerous blank spaces, taunting me as the clock ticked closer to the buzzer.

Years later, when I attended Baylor University, I selected my major by flipping through the catalog and looking for one that didn't require any math or foreign language classes. Bingo! I graduated with a recreation and leisure services degree. I remember my dad saying, "You're majoring in what?"

My dad excelled at math. It made sense to him. What didn't make sense to him was the fact that I didn't understand it. His frustration while trying to tutor me—and my frustration with him and math—occasionally built to the point that we would be yelling at each other. I usually ended up crying.

But Dad's attitude about my struggle in math about-faced at the end of my sophomore year in high school. I had been doing horribly in geometry, and I thought I was going to fail the class. When I finally received my grades, I told my dad that I had passed geometry by one point. He looked at me and said in his New York accent, "I'm proud of you, Rach!" Immediately I felt the pressure lift. Somewhere along the line, my dad had let go of his expectations and simply loved me for who I was!

His loving response affected me so much that I shared this story at my dad's funeral. His example reminds me that at times you and I may not parent well and we may make mistakes, but it's never too late to change. It's important not to stay in the same rut of sinful behavior toward our children.

Thankfully, we have a heavenly Father who always responds to us perfectly. We can rely on Him and honestly confess to Him as we parent our children, lead a company, coach a team, pastor a church, or teach a class. The more time we spend with our heavenly Father, the more we will lead like Him and be a positive influence on those around us, full of patience and life-giving words.

You may want to ask yourself these questions I've had to consider: *Am I in a rut of sin when dealing with my children? Am I packing on the pressure for my children while at the same time hurting their self-esteem because of my expectations?*

If you're not sure of the answer, you might consider a few more questions: *Am I refusing to let go of my desire for them to make the grades I expect or gain a place on the team I have in mind? Does my stress level rise to the point of anger when my children are wound up and rambunctious before bedtime? Does the sight of my children's messy rooms prompt me to berate them? When my child spills a drink in the car, do I fly off the handle?*

It's worth asking ourselves a similar question about our response to those we lead or interact with at work or at church: *Do I find myself sacrificing kindness and patience just to get a job done, hurting people along the way?*

I never thought to ask my dad what prompted his shift in perspective. Why did he stop getting angry with me over my grades? I don't really know. But I am thankful that I got to experience the change in him. The power of that moment, knowing he accepted me and loved me as I am, has stayed with me all these years.

It's not too late for any of us to change! From one day to the next, let your family, your coworkers, and your friends see a kinder and more patient person who cares more about them than the expectations driving you. The change in your attitude could be so encouraging, relief giving, and freeing that your former expectations are actually exceeded.

I am living proof. Believe it or not, in my last two years at Baylor University, I made the dean's list!

CREATING
A LEGACY OF WORKING
FOR GOD

How can you prioritize people over accomplishments today?

Be a Jesus Follower: *Release the pressure. Encourage others.*

Do not let any unwholesome talk come out of your mouths, but only what is helpful for building others up according to their needs, that it may benefit those who listen.

Ephesians 4:29

27

Faithful Caregiver

I was running late to our family meeting with my dad's nephrologist. I darted through the lobby lined with diabetic patients hunched over on benches or leaning on walkers. Some were in wheelchairs, having undergone amputations because of the neuropathy that so often sets in with diabetes.

Finally making it to the doctor's office, I opened the door and saw that my mom, my brother, and my sister were all waiting for me, along with the doctor. I sat down as he began to inform us about the state of my dad's health and what we would face in the days and months to come. Dad's kidneys were shutting down because of the effects of diabetes. If he didn't start dialysis soon, it was likely that he wouldn't survive. A thousand questions spun through my head: *Can he have a kidney transplant? . . . Will this be permanent? . . . How long can someone in his condition survive on dialysis? . . . How often will he have to go for treatments? . . . Can it be done from home? . . . Will he be able to continue with his normal activities?*

The doctor, who was a Jesus Follower and a friend of the family, did his best to answer all our questions. Dad wouldn't be a candidate for a kidney transplant, because of his poor health and age. Dialysis would be a part of the rest of his life. That hit me hard. My basic understanding was that three days a week my dad would have to go to a dialysis center to have his blood cleansed. Because he was a big man, home dialysis was not an option. The entire process sounded barbaric, and I was just hoping and praying my dad would agree to it.

My mom was amazing that day. She stayed focused, she asked really good questions, she took notes, she never fell to pieces, and she took charge—which is exactly what she would have to do from that point on. She had now become the caregiver. My mom had been a young bride at eighteen, marrying a twenty-nine-year-old man. I am sure she didn't realize at the time what that age difference would mean years down the road. Not that it would have changed her mind. But God had a plan all along, and as difficult as the road ahead would be for my mom and dad, God would use it in both of their lives to increase their faith and reliance on Him.

My dad endured dialysis three days a week for six years before he went to be with Jesus. The doctor never projected that he would live that long. Many people live for years on dialysis, but my dad was seventy-two years old and in poor health. The doctor said that people in his condition usually manage to survive on dialysis anywhere from six months to three years. But always the competitor, my dad pushed himself to remain physically and mentally strong.

My mom dreaded the moment when she would have to take the car keys away from him. She even had the doctor talk to him, hoping the doctor would deliver that unwelcome news, but he chickened out! Still, God was faithful. After Dad had a small stroke, he went to rehab following his hospitalization. There he was told that he couldn't drive for six weeks after he returned home. Mom seized the opportunity and just never gave the keys back to Dad. In time, he accepted the fact that others would drive him wherever he wanted to go. My mom made sure she remained available so that he never had to ask twice if he wanted her to take him somewhere.

Mom quickly realized that she would need help getting Dad to dialysis and to his Bible studies. While she was happy to do the runs back and forth to the clinic, as Dad became weaker, she worried that she wouldn't be able to steady him if he tripped or began to fall. Once again, God met her need for help by placing her on the hearts of some of Dad's Bible study buddies. These businessmen, coaches, and pastors all loved my dad and were very loyal to him. They could see he was growing weaker and harder to handle physically. So they offered to be his Transportation Team. They each signed up for one of the six weekly runs to and from the dialysis center. They did this faithfully for the last three years of Dad's life. The guys who opted for the early-morning runs showed up promptly at 6:15 a.m. They helped him out the door of the house, then prayed with him in the car before walking him into the clinic. The men who signed up for the noon runs either picked up lunch for him on the way home or took him to lunch. He loved the fellowship they provided. They truly ministered to Dad's spirit as they provided a meaningful practical service. Dad had spent years investing in their lives, and now they wanted to give back. They were patient when he was quiet or not feeling well, and they encouraged him with their stories and with Bible verses.

Mom couldn't have done it without those guys. They gave her a much-needed break even if it was just for a few minutes. To this day, she keeps in her sunroom a signed picture of these ten men, taken at Dad's funeral, where they served as pallbearers.

After my dad had been on dialysis for three years, one morning in my mom's devotions God spoke to her through Scripture. He said, "Go, my people, enter your rooms and shut the doors behind you; hide yourselves for a little while."[1] My mom said it felt as if the verse had leaped off the page. She knew God was telling her to step back from ministry for a time, and she immediately obeyed. While she fulfilled engagements she had already committed to, she declined all those that were pending. I so appreciate that my mom is in ministry not to promote herself but to do God's will. So when He told her to back off ministry for a time and stay at home, she said, "Yes Sir."

Almost immediately my dad's health plummeted. Those last three years of his life were packed full of emergency situations, 911 calls, and twenty-four-hour care from my mom. The Lord knew that Dad would need her full-time care, something she would never have been able to provide if she had continued traveling and speaking.

During those three difficult years, I saw my mom on her knees, scrubbing blood from the carpet when my dad's fistula didn't clot properly following dialysis or when the bandage was removed too soon. Such situations were deeply unsettling, because a lot of blood can be lost in a matter of minutes. And even a small amount of blood makes quite a scary mess.

My mom, who was used to speaking on stages, sitting in green rooms waiting for TV interviews, and eating dinners with presidents and dignitaries all over the world, was now cleaning up messes, scrubbing blood out of clothes, calling 911 every couple of months, talking with doctors, waiting in the ER, and sorting through pills. She also took the brunt of my dad's emotional roller coasters brought on by fluctuations in his blood sugar levels. I don't know whether my dad recognized how angry he seemed at such times. On the hard days, when my dad wasn't feeling well and his blood sugar levels were out of whack, he took his frustration out on my mom with an impatient remark or blamed her for losing something he had misplaced. I can still hear him yelling, "Anne, where did you hide my hearing aids?" To this day, when we lose something, we laugh as we blame "Anne."

I am in no way wanting to disrespect my dad; I just want to get across the point that at times he wasn't the easiest to be around and my mom had more challenges than just physical labor in caring for him. Thankfully, the Lord in His sovereignty created my mom to not be overly emotional. She is made of really tough stuff. She would have been a great athlete. She handled the emotional stress like a champ. Mom never cowered or gave in to frustration. She stood her ground and continued serving him with joy.

Of course, Dad's mood shifts weren't the only thing taking an emotional toll on Mom as his caregiver. I lost count of how many times my dad visited the emergency room. I know he was in the hospital for the last eight Decembers. Mom joked with the nurses that going to the hospital had become one of our Christmas traditions. But the visits were serious. Each time, we didn't know whether he would make it back out. Each time, he emerged weaker than before. Many times he had to transition to rehab in order to regain enough strength to come home.

One December the dialysis clinic had difficulty accessing his port, so without telling Mom, they sent him straight to a surgical clinic. The clinic put in a new port that, unbeknownst to us, became infected. On a Sunday morning, Mom found Dad delirious with a 104-degree fever. He was rushed to the hospital, where the new port had to be removed. It was terrifying for us to learn that he had MRSA, a staph infection that is resistant to antibiotics and is deadly if it travels to the brain or heart. Mom sent a desperate SOS email to his men's Bible study groups, asking for prayer. The email went viral, and tens of thousands of people started to pray.

I know the doctors didn't think he would survive, but they didn't know my warrior dad. After many infusions of antibiotics, he was finally moved to rehab. But Christmas Day was quickly approaching, and my mom wasn't about to let him sit in rehab during our family's most special day of the year. After much spirited discussion with the medical staff, she convinced them to allow Dad to leave for just the day. He was so happy to be surrounded by love and family. He was exhausted, of course, but he sat and watched all of us and listened and laughed. I believe it fueled his determination to get stronger. Not long afterward, he was released to come home.

We all loved Dad, and our hearts ached to see this giant of a man reduced to needles and syringes, finger pricks, way-too-small hospital gowns, walkers, nausea from dialysis, extreme tiredness, hiccups that lasted for three days at a time, and laryngospasms that left him unable to breathe for what seemed like forever. Yet most of the time he managed to maintain a sense of humor, as did my mom, who made it her goal to keep him comfortable, fed, rested, and free from worries. In no way would my dad have made it as long as he did without her thorough care. She became his doctor, his nurse, his pharmacist, his coach, his driver, his cook, his laundress, his cleaner, his encourager, his counselor, his advocate, his prayer warrior, his shoulder to lean on. She did it all. Never do I remember her wanting to give up. She took care of him without sleep, without any thought to herself. She was able to do it because she never neglected her time with the Lord each day. God sustained her.

And God also knew when it was enough.

My dad passed away about the time we started looking for a nursing home facility for him. We could tell that he had reached a point where Mom would no longer be able to care for him herself, yet we knew that Dad would resist going to a care facility, and we really didn't want to send him. I am so thankful he never even knew we were looking. We experienced the beauty of God's sovereign timing, even in death.

The pain and hard work of being Dad's caregiver is over for my mom, but she has most certainly reaped crowns in Heaven for her service. She loved taking care of my dad, as ornery as he could be at times. This powerful woman of God, who can preach the Word like no one else, demonstrated true power as she took joy in serving my dad in everyday, humble ways. I saw that her attitude was "the same as that of Christ Jesus: Who, being in very nature God, did not consider equality with God something to be grasped, but made himself nothing, taking the very nature of a servant."[2]

When they exchanged vows on their wedding day, Mom and Dad said, "Until death do us part." Not "As long as you make me happy." Not "As long as you make my life easier." Not "Until I get tired of you." Watching my parents reminded me that marriage isn't something to discard, no matter how hard it gets. It's a covenant made before God.

My mom's example has also shown me that God has a much deeper purpose in marriage than just fulfilling needs or providing a companion. He uses it to shape us into people who reflect Jesus. In fact, that's how He uses all the difficulties of life.

It's in the hardest times, especially in our relationships, that God does the most work. Hebrews 6:10 suggests that we show our love for God when we help His people. Our work of caring for others, in whatever capacity God calls us, will not go unrewarded. So let's be faithful caregivers at every opportunity.

CREATING A LEGACY OF WORKING FOR GOD

In what challenging situation can you seek to demonstrate a servant's heart and offer the care someone needs?

Be a Jesus Follower: *Serve others with compassion.*

The Son of Man did not come to be served, but to serve, and to give his life as a ransom for many.

Matthew 20:28

28

Kentucky Arena

I am sure there are days when you feel sapped of all strength, utterly unable to serve God in the capacity to which He's called you. Could it be the enemy trying to get you to quit? Have you considered quitting, believing you are justified in doing so?

I don't know what your situation or your calling is, but I know from watching my mother that God equips you for whatever He's called you to do, even on days when you feel like you can't.

I'll never forget one particular example of Mom's perseverance under circumstances that would have caused most people to quit. I was six months pregnant and had left my fourteen-month-old at home while I attended my mother's Just Give Me Jesus revival in Lexington, Kentucky. The Rupp Arena was packed during that Saturday morning session, and I was seated two rows up from the arena floor, facing the cross-shaped podium. With my Bible open on my lap, I listened intently as my mom gave her message. I can't help but get sucked in when she speaks, because she delivers her message with such riveting authority and passion. She makes the Bible come alive. I love that she's never fluffy or cheesy or overly dramatic. Sometimes you listen to speakers and wonder whether they are thinking about their next facial expression instead of the message they are giving. When my mom speaks, you know she has come fully prepared in study, in prayer, and in focus. This day was no different, and it was powerful. The entire arena audience was as riveted as I was.

At one moment, as she was explaining Jesus's command "Feed my sheep" from John 21,[1] my mother suddenly gripped the side of the podium and put one hand on her mouth. I shot to the edge of my seat. She mumbled what sounded like "Please give me a minute." Then she began to slowly collapse! My brother-in-law and her security guard miraculously made it to the podium in time to catch her just before she hit the stage floor. They then carried her off the stage and laid her down on the cold concrete of the arena floor, which brought her to consciousness.

Without even thinking, I handed my Bible to the person next to me. Grasping the railing, I launched my rather large pregnant body over it and onto the arena floor. As I ran toward the stage, my sister came up beside me. We couldn't get near Mom because of the throng of people who surrounded her. If you've ever passed out, you know that nothing is worse than when you regain consciousness and open your eyes to tons of faces staring at you. Faces that you may or may not know, asking a million questions like "Are you okay?" "How many fingers am I holding up?" and "Does anything hurt?"—which only serves to make you feel more nauseated and sweat more profusely. My sister and I pressed through the crowd, hoping to get close enough for Mom to see us and at least know that we were praying.

As we stood there silently praying, I heard something. I tapped Morrow's arm, which was tightly interwoven with mine, and said, "Listen." The sound of thousands of voices praying echoed throughout the arena. Some were close enough that we could hear them praying for God to restore Mom and heal her. Then Fernando Ortega, the worship leader, led the audience in a hymn, which we later learned Mom had asked him to do while she was lying on the floor of the arena.

I kept my arm around Morrow as we tried to shimmy through the crowd. Never before had my mother passed out onstage. We were ter-rified, but I could feel the prayers helping me stay calm. I remember whispering to Morrow, as tears streamed down her face, that with all this prayer, Mom was going to be okay. We finally saw her shakily sipping Coke through a straw (her favorite). I heard her say she was going to get back up on the platform. Apparently over one hundred people had called 911, so the EMS crew arrived quickly. The gurney was waiting, and the paramedics were ready to cart her off. No one would have argued. In fact, I am sure every person in the arena would have understood. But my mother emphatically stated in a weak voice, "I am going back up there. Just please get me a chair to sit in on the platform." Meanwhile, I was thinking, *She's going to do what?*

The amazing thing is that such determination is not out of char-acter for my mom. She would have chewed up and spit out any-body who dared to argue with her in that moment, because it was so important to her to finish the work she had been given. She lives, eats, and breathes her love for and devotion to Christ.

I'd seen this same devotion in Daddy Bill, who, at ninety-five years of age, could no longer walk, had difficulty seeing because of macular degeneration, and had difficulty hearing, yet worked hard to share his hope on video. Then God used that video to bring tens of thousands of people to faith in Christ.[2]

So, too, nothing would derail Mom's service to the Lord. She didn't climb back up on the platform to please the crowd, she didn't climb back up on the platform to draw attention to herself, she didn't climb back up on the platform to defy the EMS guys, and she didn't climb back up on the platform to prove she was tough as nails. She climbed back up on the platform because she knew that God's will for her that day was to tell an arena full of people about Jesus. She wouldn't allow the enemy to keep her from carrying out the call God had given her, even if she felt like curl-ing up in a deep hole. She is more devoted to Jesus than anyone I know.

If I had been in my mom's place, I would have probably said something like "Take me home! I know God allowed this for a rea-son, and He knows I have no strength now. I can't possibly get back up there." Many of us would have done our best to mask our humiliation. If my mom had chosen to do that, no one would have blamed her or even questioned her. But what an opportunity she would have missed!

We know this because my mom did get back up on the stage. She stood shakily and climbed up the stairs to her chair. Her voice was much softer, and her strength was obviously gone, but God enabled her to finish her message. What a legacy!

When my mom finished speaking, she walked backstage, refusing those who insisted she ride in a wheelchair. My sister and I sat together, waiting for a doctor to come and give my mom a quick evaluation before her next message.[3] (Yes, she still had two more sessions to lead. And after a lunch break, she did!)

The black curtain separating the room from the stage parted, and a security guard came in quietly with several other members of my mom's ministry team. He was the same man who had jumped onstage when Mom fainted. He said that as my mom was blacking out and sliding to the floor, he heard her say over and over in a quiet voice, with her eyes closed, "Feed My lambs; feed My lambs; feed My lambs." Barely able to speak, trying to contain his tears, the man, who was not only part of her security but also an executive pastor, said he would never forget the strength of her obedience to her calling—to give God's Word to God's people—even as she was slipping into unconsciousness.

By her example, I am challenged to never quit before I finish the assignment God has given me. Oh, that our half-conscious words and thoughts would be not about ourselves but about our love for Christ and those He's given us to instruct.

Don't give up! Let's be living, breathing examples of men and women who serve and obey God at all costs. Because we love Him and to do anything else would be absurd.

CREATING
A LEGACY OF WORKING
FOR GOD

Ask God to give you an unshakable commitment to share the hope of the gospel until your final breath.

Be a Jesus Follower: *Don't quit. Ever.*

Jesus said to Simon Peter, "Simon son of John, do you truly love me more than these?" "Yes, Lord," he said, "you know that I love you." Jesus said, "Feed my lambs."

John 21:15

CONCLUSION

Running the Race

Noah received the Baton of Truth that started its journey with Adam and Eve and was passed on by each successive generation until it reached him. He preserved it; then it was passed on in an unbroken line to Jesus, the Messiah.[1] Noah was truly a gold medal winner in the race of life.

Noah handed the Baton to Shem, who passed it to Eber, to Terah, to Abraham, to Isaac . . . Jacob . . . Joseph . . . Moses . . . Joshua . . . Deborah . . . Gideon . . . Samson . . . Ruth . . . Samuel . . . David . . . Solomon . . . Elijah . . . Elisha . . . Hezekiah . . . Josiah . . . Haggai . . . Zechariah . . . Ezra . . . Nehemiah . . . Malachi . . . to John the Baptist, who received the Baton of Truth and passed it by bearing witness to "the Lamb of God, who takes away the sin of the world!"[2] And for a short while, once again, people's faith became sight as they gazed on God face to face in the person of Jesus of Nazareth! John the apostle rejoiced as he exclaimed, "We have seen his glory, the glory of the one and only Son, who came from the Father, full of grace and truth."[3]

John the apostle received the Baton of Truth directly from Jesus Christ. He then passed it by faith to Polycarp, an early-church leader who heard John say he had seen God in the flesh, in Christ. Polycarp received the Baton, and before he was burned at the stake for his faith, he passed it to Ambrose, who passed it to Augustine, to Anselm, to John Wycliffe, to John Huss . . . Martin Luther . . . John Calvin . . . John Knox . . . John Bunyan . . . Jonathan Edwards . . . John Wesley . . . George Whitefield . . . Francis Asbury . . . William Carey . . . Charles Haddon Spurgeon . . . Dwight L. Moody . . . I. M. Haldeman . . . Billy Sunday . . . William Franklin Graham Sr. . . . Billy Graham . . . to Anne Graham Lotz, who passed it to Rachel-Ruth Lotz Wright, who now relays it to you.

Now the passing of the Baton is up to you.

Think about it. The Baton of Truth was received face to face and then relayed faith to faith from generation to generation. But it's the same Baton . . . the same Truth . . . the same good news . . . the same gospel . . . that God loves you! He wants you to know Him in a personal relationship. Your sin has separated you from Him, but you can enter into relationship with Him through the sacrifice of the Lamb, whose blood was shed on the cross to make atonement for your sin. The only way to safety . . . the only way into God's ark . . . the only way to have a right relationship with God is through the blood of the Lamb, the Son of God, even the Lord Jesus Christ. But everyone is invited to enter. Whosoever will may come. And when you come, your sins are forgiven. You have the hope of Heaven when you die. You have a right relationship with God. You have eternal life. You have Jesus. That's the gospel.

Now it's up to you: Would you make sure you have received and are firmly gripping the Baton of Truth?

Rachel-Ruth and I are praying that God will use this book to give you a vision for everyone within your sphere of influence to experience the same certainty of God's love, forgiveness, and welcome that you have. Then run your race by witnessing for God and worshipping God and walking with God and working for God as you pass the Baton to the next generation!

Don't drop the Baton. Don't even bobble it. It's been passed to you through all the generations of human history. Receive it as the treasure that it is, and then pass it on to someone else.

Therefore,

since we are surrounded by such a great cloud of witnesses,

let us throw off everything that hinders and the sin

that so easily entangles,

and let us run with perseverance the race marked out for us.

Let us fix our eyes on Jesus.

Hebrews 12:1–2

At the Starting Line

I f, in reading *Jesus Followers,* you have come to the conclusion that you are not on the running team . . .

If you cannot remember a time when you intentionally received the Baton of Truth . . .

If you have never deliberately come inside the ark . . .

then the two of us invite you to do so now.

Pray a simple prayer, something like this:

Dear God,

I want to receive the Baton. I want to make sure I'm in the ark, saved from Your judgment. So right now I come to the cross by faith and confess I'm a sinner.[1] I was born that way. I'm a son of Adam. I'm a daughter of Eve. I'm asking You to forgive me of my sin as I turn away from it.[2] I claim the blood of Jesus to cover me, to cleanse me.[3] I ask that You forgive me in His name. And I believe Jesus died for me.[4] If there had been no one else who needed to be saved, He would have died just for me. I receive the Baton of Truth for myself. I believe Jesus rose from the dead to give me eternal life, which I understand is a personal relationship with You right now and a heavenly Home when I die.[5] I open my heart and invite Jesus to come live inside me in the person of the Holy Spirit.[6] I surrender my life to Him as Lord. From this moment forward, I will run my race, fixing my eyes on Jesus, following Him . . . all the way Home.[7]

For the glory of His name,
Amen.

If you prayed the above prayer in sincere faith, then your sins are forgiven. You have received eternal life. Heaven is your home. God is your Father. You no longer have to struggle through life, running your race on your own. God is with you. He is for you. He loves you! You are now the Father's child. Welcome to His family!

To encourage you as you begin running the race, we want to share one more story. It took place at the 1992 Barcelona Summer Olympics and powerfully illustrates the incredible courage, perseverance, and help that are sometimes required to finish the race.

A British sprinter, Derek Redmond, qualified for the semifinal of the four-hundred-meter race with the fastest time in his heat. He was running very strong in the semifinal when he suddenly pulled up with an agonized cry. He had torn his hamstring! Instead of crumpling to the ground, Derek continued to hobble as he desperately tried to finish the race. It was heart stopping. Heart wrenching. The audience was transfixed by what was taking place on the track. Suddenly a man rushed out of the stands, brushed aside security, put his arms around Derek, and supported him to the finish line. The man? Derek's father![8]

The race that you have now begun to run can be hard. Grueling. Painful. Especially when something interrupts or crushes your efforts, hopes, and dreams, such as when you do your best to pass the Baton to a loved one yet the Truth is rejected, when your spouse walks out of the marriage for no clear reason, when your health is threatened by a deadly disease, when your child dies long before his time, when your job is lost or your career crumbles, or when your savings evaporate so that you face old age with very little to live on.

But please hear us, dear reader. Now that you belong to God's family, He is your loving Father. While He may not protect you from "tearing your hamstring," He promises to be right there to put His arms around you, comfort you, strengthen you, and help you cross the finish line.[9] Yes, He will. Rachel-Ruth and I both know. We are His children, and we know we can trust our Father's love to provide all we need in order to finish the race.

> To him who is able to keep you from falling
> and to present you before his glorious presence
> without fault and with great joy—
> to the only God our Savior
> be glory, majesty, power and authority,
> through
> Jesus Christ our Lord,
> before all ages, now and forevermore!
> Amen.
>
> Jude 24–25

ACKNOWLEDGMENTS

As we've written this book together, some people have stood out as those we want to especially acknowledge.

The first person who comes to our minds is the one you know as Ruth Bell Graham but the one Rachel-Ruth knows as Tai Tai and the one Anne knows as Mother. Her spiritual depth, her sharp wit, her rollicking sense of humor, her unconditional love for each of her children, grandchildren, and great-grandchildren, and her consistent walk with Jesus have made a deep impact on us both.

The lives of the primary characters in this book have compelled us to grasp the Baton of Truth for ourselves, run our race, and then pass the Baton to the next generation. We are deeply grateful.

We also want to acknowledge those in the next generation who are already reaching for the Baton, eager to pass it to others. Rachel-Ruth's three daughters, Anne's three granddaughters, are seeking to faithfully run their race to the praise of God's glory. Bell, Sophia, and Riggin, to whom this book is dedicated, have been patient, helpful, and insightful and have provided both of us with joy. They are channels of God's blessing in our family.

Because this is our first book together, we want to thank Tina Constable and our Multnomah family for believing in us and giving us this opportunity. We also would never have been able to express ourselves clearly and concisely without the expert editing pen of Laura Barker. We have both been richly blessed by everyone we have worked with in marketing, publicity, design, sales, and so many other areas.

And we are delighted to share with you pictures from our family album. Thank you, Charlene Ochoa, for helping gather them, then making multiple runs to the photo shop to get them into HD quality. We hope you, as a reader, enjoy the pictures and find that they enhance the stories.

Last, we want to thank you for picking up this book. Our prayer is that you will recommit yourself to grasping the Baton of Truth for yourself and passing it to those of the next generation.

NOTES

Genesis 5 | The Beginning of the Race

1. Genesis 5, NKJV.

PART ONE | Our Witness

1. Genesis 3:5.
2. Genesis 3:22.
3. Colossians 1:16.
4. Hebrews 9:22.
5. John 1:29.
6. Genesis 3:15; Hebrews 10:4.
7. My maternal grandfather's name was L. Nelson Bell. He became the moderator of the Presbyterian Church in the United States the year before he died. He helped found the *Presbyterian Journal* and *Christianity Today.*
8. Genesis 4:3–4.
9. Genesis 4:6–9.
10. 1 Peter 3:15.
11. Hebrews 11:4.
12. Genesis 4:25.

1 | Making the Most of Every Opportunity

1. Luke 6:45.
2. The story is true, but the name has been changed for privacy.

2 | Popcorn and Chocolate Milk

1. Hebrews 4:15, NKJV.

5 | Hidden Treasures

1. Revelation 12:10, KJV.

6 | A Reflection of God's Faithful Love

1. Ephesians 5:22–33.
2. Genesis 1:28: "God blessed them and said to them, 'Be fruitful and increase in number; fill the earth and subdue it.'" The very first command God gave Adam and Eve was to be fruitful.
3. Psalm 3:3.
4. 1 Corinthians 13:5.

7 | Embracing the Fullness of God's Family

1. John 3:16.
2. 1 Samuel 16:7.

PART TWO | Our Worship

1. Genesis 4:10–12, 23–24; 6:1–3.
2. Genesis 4:26.
3. For more on this, please see Anne Graham Lotz, *Wounded by God's People: Discovering How God's Love Heals Our Hearts* (Grand Rapids, MI: Zondervan, 2013).
4. John 4:24.
5. Ephesians 1:22–23.
6. Revelation 4:6, 8–10.
7. Revelation 5:11–13.
8. Revelation 5:12.

8 | A Love for the Word

1. Revelation 3:8.

9 | The View from the Top

1. Matthew 17:1.
2. Housefires, "Good, Good Father," by Anthony Brown and Pat Barrett, *Housefires II*, Housefires, 2014.

10 | Seek Ye First

1. Matthew 6:33, KJV.
2. Isaiah 43:19.

11 | Fiddlesticks

1. Nettie Hutson, "Are You Shining?," adapted from the hymn "Are You Shining for the Master?," 1913, https://hymnary.org/text /are_you_shining_for_the_master.

12 | Praise in the Midst of Pain

1. John 19:26–27; Luke 23:39–43.

PART THREE | Our Walk

1. Genesis 5:2.
2. Jude 14–15.
3. Genesis 5:22.
4. Genesis 4:20–22.
5. Genesis 5:24, NKJV.
6. Enoch is one of two Old Testament men who did not die. Elijah is the other one.
7. Martin Rogers, "Why U.S. Team Was Disqualified in Men's 4x100 Relay," *USA Today*, August 20, 2016, www.usatoday.com/story /sports/olympics/rio-2016/2016/08/19/united-states-men-4x100 -meter-relay-disqualification-explanation/89032360.

15 | Breaking Bread and Making Memories

1. Grampa Lotz pastored small churches in the Bronx and never took a salary. What the church gave him, he put back into the offering plate. He worked for the New York Telephone Company to provide for his family, so his calls to us were free of charge. In fact, when Mom and Dad got married, he called Mom five times a day! Dad had to ask him to cut back from calling so much.

18 | Red-Flag Warnings

1. 2 Kings 4:4.
2. Psalm 23:3.

19 | Set Apart

1. As my mom went over this chapter with me, she told me something I had not known previously. She said that at White House state dinners, at meals with the Queen of England, or in other notable circumstances, Tai Tai and Daddy Bill had come to an agreement about the wine that was served. In order to be gracious guests, Tai Tai would accept a glass of wine, and Daddy Bill would abstain. On the other hand, my parents have also been at incredibly important functions, including a dinner at the Tower of London hosted by Princess Margaret. But both of my parents have always abstained without hesitation.

2. Christopher Ingraham, "America's Biggest Drug Threat Is 100% Legal," *Washington Post,* March 28, 2016, www.washingtonpost .com/news/wonk/wp/2016/03/28/americas-biggest-drug-threat -is-100-legal; Joshua M. Masino, "Drinking vs. Drugs: Alcohol Is Still America's Number One Problem," AddictionBlog.org, November 4, 2017, https://alcohol.addictionblog.org/drinking -vs-drugs-alcohol-is-still-americas-number-one-problem.

3. Brian Obodeze, "Alcohol and Crime: Does the Popular Drug Influence Offence Levels?," AlcoRehab.org, https://alcorehab .org/the-effects-of-alcohol/alcohol-related-crimes.

4. "Teen Drivers: Get the Facts," CDC, November 18, 2020, www.cdc.gov/transportationsafety/teen_drivers/teendrivers _factsheet.html.

5. Romans 14:7, 13, 21.

6. Luke 17:1–3.

7. Romans 12:2; 2 Timothy 2:21.

20 | Pursuing Purity

1. Psalm 119:9.

2. 2 Samuel 11:1–17.

3. Daniel 1:8, NKJV.

4. Psalm 101:3.

21 | Love Stories

1. See chapter 5, "Hidden Treasures."

22 | Facing Death

1. Psalm 3:3.
2. Isaiah 35:3.
3. Matthew 5:4.
4. Psalm 34:18.
5. John 14:2.
6. Fanny J. Crosby, "Blessed Assurance," 1873, public domain.
7. 2 Corinthians 5:1.
8. 1 Thessalonians 4:13.

PART FOUR | Our Work

1. Genesis 5:29.
2. Genesis 6:5–7.
3. Genesis 6:13–14.
4. Genesis 6:22.
5. 2 Peter 2:5.
6. Genesis 7:21–23.
7. 2 Peter 3:9.
8. John 3:16.
9. Acts 4:12.
10. John 14:6.

23 | The World Awaits

1. Cover, *Time*, May 16, 1994, http://content.time.com/time /magazine/0,9263,7601940516,00.html.

25 | Full Attention

1. 1 Peter 3:12.

27 | Faithful Caregiver

1. Isaiah 26:20.
2. Philippians 2:5–7.

28 | Kentucky Arena

1. John 21:17.
2. This video can be found at www.youtube.com/watch?v=bba2Dqaw6SI.

3. The doctor's evaluation and subsequent tests Mom went through when she returned home revealed no reason for her collapse. She believes to this day that the enemy had wanted to take her out. But praise God! He did not! The afternoon sessions were powerful, and the audience was totally engaged, comprehending that my mother was not performing but just giving them Jesus.

CONCLUSION | Running the Race

1. Luke 3:23–38.
2. John 1:29.
3. John 1:14.

APPENDIX | At the Starting Line

1. Romans 3:23.
2. 1 John 1:9.
3. Ephesians 1:7.
4. Romans 5:8.
5. John 1:12; 14:2–3.
6. Galatians 4:6; Revelation 3:20.
7. Hebrews 12:1–2.
8. Olympics, "Derek Redmond's Inspirational 400m Race at Barcelona 1992: Throwback Thursday," April 9, 2020, YouTube video, www.youtube.com/watch?v=yrboO72eJKg.
9. Psalm 23:4; Isaiah 41:10.

ABOUT THE AUTHORS

Called "the best preacher in the family" by her late father, Billy Graham, ANNE GRAHAM LOTZ speaks around the globe with the wisdom and authority of years spent studying God's Word.

The *New York Times* named Anne one of the five most influential evangelists of her generation. Her Just Give Me Jesus revivals have been held in more than thirty cities in twelve countries, with hundreds of thousands of attendees.

Anne is a bestselling and award-winning author of nineteen books. She is the president of AnGeL Ministries in Raleigh, North Carolina, and served as chairperson of the National Day of Prayer Task Force from 2016 to 2017.

Whether a delegate to the World Economic Forum's annual meeting, a commentator in the *Washington Post,* or a groundbreaking speaker on platforms throughout the world, Anne's aim is clear: to bring revival to the hearts of God's people. And her message is consistent: calling people into a personal relationship with God through His Word.

RACHEL-RUTH LOTZ WRIGHT is a graduate of Baylor University. She is married to Steven Wright, a high school football head coach, and they have three wonderful teenage daughters who have given her a heart for children and for those who raise them. God opened the door for her to speak at schools, churches, and other venues across the country to share the gospel with kids and also to ignite in parents a desire to raise disciples who love God's Word.

For the past eight years, Rachel-Ruth has been teaching a weekly Bible study, which recently moved online and now draws a global audience of thousands. It is her desire that people, no matter their age, would be drawn into a vibrant love relationship with the Lord through His Word.

Rachel-Ruth holds the position of ministry teaching associate at AnGeL Ministries, serves on the AnGeL Ministries board of directors, and chairs the weekly prayer team that undergirds her mother's ministry. Rachel-Ruth and her family live in Raleigh, North Carolina.

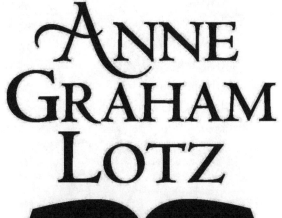

AnGeL Ministries

5115 Hollyridge Drive

Raleigh, NC 27612-3111

(919) 787-6606

info@AnneGrahamLotz.org

COMFORTER. COUNSELOR. FRIEND.

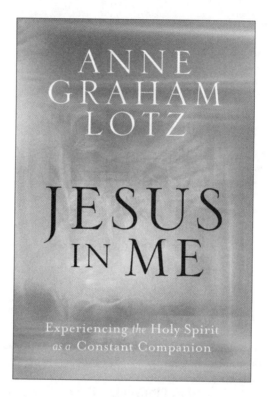

We may know something about God and something about Jesus, but what do we know about the Holy Spirit? Too often, we seem to overlook the third person of the Trinity, perhaps because we don't know much about Him. He seems mystical; reserved for superspiritual Christians. We might even say He intimidates us—or somehow seems optional.

In *Jesus in Me,* Anne Graham Lotz draws on her rich biblical knowledge as well as her personal story—including her cancer diagnosis—to help us understand that the Holy Spirit is not a magic genie, a flame of fire, or a vague feeling. He is a person who prays for us, guides us in our relationships and decisions, comforts us in pain, and stays by our side at all times. He is not an optional extra in the Christian life; He is a divine necessity. In this simple yet profound teaching, she explores seven key aspects of the Holy Spirit that will revolutionize how you understand and relate to this vital member of the Trinity.

Discover how you can better love and rely on the person of the Holy Spirit—and embrace how much He loves you.

MULTNOMAH

waterbrookmultnomah.com

OPEN YOUR HEART
TO GOD'S INVITATION
TO PRAYER

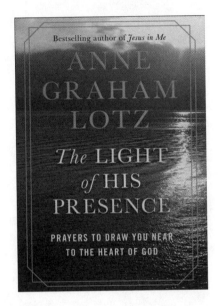

Why is it that as soon as we bow our heads to pray, we start thinking of other things we need to do? How do we make time to pray in the middle of our busy lives? And how do we know what to say and how to say it?

Like many of us, Anne Graham Lotz has struggled with prayer. Over the years, she discovered that writing out her prayers draws her into deeper, more intimate conversations with God. *The Light of His Presence* offers forty of these tender, honest prayers for real-life situations as an invitation to deepen your own prayer life through worship, confession, thanksgiving, and intercession. You'll be encouraged to lean more fully into God's promises through this power-packed devotional resource, which includes inspiring quotes from Christians throughout the ages and also has space to journal your own words to God.

As Anne writes, "My prayer for you as you read this volume is that God will use my struggle with prayer to help you overcome yours. And that, as a result, you will be drawn nearer to the heart of God."

MULTNOMAH

waterbrookmultnomah.com